PLAYING
Second
FIDDLE

God's Heart for
Harmony Regarding Women
and the Church

JUDI PEERS

Printed in Canada

ISBN: 978-1-4866-0727-3

Word Alive Press
131 Cordite Road, Winnipeg, MB R3W 1S1
www.wordalivepress.ca

WORD ALIVE
—P R E S S—

Library and Archives Canada Cataloguing in Publication

Peers, Judi, 1956-, author

　　　Playing second fiddle : God's heart for harmony regarding

women and the church / Judi Peers.

Issued in print and electronic formats.

ISBN 978-1-4866-0727-3 (pbk.).--ISBN 978-1-4866-0728-0

(pdf).--ISBN 978-1-4866-0729-7 (html).--ISBN 978-1-4866-0730-3

(epub)

　　　1. Christian women--Religious life. I. Title.

BV4527.P43 2014　　　　　　248.8'43　　　　　　C2014-906973-1

　　　　　　　　　　　　　　　　　　　　　　　C2014-906974-X

For my grandbabies—
Weston Jones Wade,
who plunged headfirst
into the river of life on May 28, 2013

and

Archie David Peers,
whose midnight arrival on Great-Grandma's
ninety-seventh birthday (June 20th, 2014)
was heralded by the great blue heron.

May you forever follow Jesus' footsteps
and discover how to treat the women in your life.

TABLE OF CONTENTS

ACKNOWLEDGEMENTS

I am eternally grateful to my parents, Lloyd and Dorothy West, my grandparents, Velma and Percy West and Clarence and Ethel Buttars, as well as my great-grandparents (particularly Herbert Davey), for their prayers and for bequeathing to me a strong legacy of faith. And to my six brothers, Gary, John, Jim, Ray, Rob and Dave, for never treating me like second fiddle.

Thanks to my immediate family as well, my husband Dave and my children and their spouses (Stephen and Laura, Sarah and Clayton, Michael and Yasmine), for loving and supporting me, and coming to the aid of their technically impaired spouse/mother. I promise I will become more computer literate in the near future.

Thank you to my faithful friends and my ladies prayer group for your friendship, prayers, and your valued input into my projects. I hesitate to name you all in fear I forget someone.

I am particularly indebted to Pastor Karl House, Doctor Brian Stiller, author Tim Huff and publisher Larry Willard of Castle Quay Books, for generously sharing their work with my readers. Blessings on you all for your supportive, second-fiddle hearts!

A huge heartfelt thank you goes to internationally acclaimed wildlife artist and author Kelly Dodge for making available her remarkable gouache painting "Rise to Greet the Sun" for our cover image. The symbolic nuances of this work are in perfect pitch with this project.

And thank you too, to Mary Coles for rescuing me close to the wire with several illustrations to augment the quotations. I.O.U.

To Jen, Amy, Evan and the team at Word Alive Press. You guys are the best! You made this an enjoyable and painless process. Although we didn't always agree on every issue, we always worked in harmonious accord. I look forward to working with you again.

Most of all, thanks be to God for revealing His heart for His precious daughters, of which I am one, and for His amazing presence and guidance through the publishing process. May we all be inspired by this revelation from the King of Kings to pick up the "bow" and play His tune.

You know, sometimes you just gotta stand up and play.
—Chris Tomlin, musician and worship leader

one

AN UNEXPECTED ASSIGNMENT

For the first time in my life, I'm wearing earplugs. There's much to love about our new location and this quaint brick house, but the master bedroom is located near the front sidewalk and the street noise penetrates: the rumble of cement mixers and lumber-delivery trucks en route to the new subdivision, the first runs of Trent University's East Bank bus, the incessant buzz of early morning traffic.

Late nights are also disturbed by a discordant mingling of sound. My youngest son, Michael, a university student, rattles about in the adjoining kitchen at odd hours. Emergency vehicles race up Armour Road, sirens screaming for attention, and occasionally a small group of late-night/early-morning revellers make their way home from the bars of downtown Peterborough. And did I mention that my husband snores?

My natural bent towards insomnia doesn't help the sleep situation. Fortunately, several years ago I came to realize that perhaps God allowed this affliction in my life for His Kingdom purposes. While lying in bed one night at our previous home, literally seconds after I closed my eyes (well before I fell asleep), God revealed to me in a glorious vision the incredible power of intercessory prayer. At first, I couldn't identify the two men involved; both faces were distant, one far to the left in my mind's eye, the other far to the right. As they moved closer to one another and closer to me, I noticed the lips of the man on the right moving in an exaggerated manner. Eventually, I was able to identify the men. On the left was my eldest son, Stephen, who had been in a horrific car accident the previous year. My father, Lloyd West, who had died of bone cancer when Stephen was in kindergarten, was on the right. When the two faces met, my dad, lips still in motion, bent slightly forward and kissed the forehead of my son. Immediately, the Spirit of God interpreted the vision: "It was the prayers of your father that kept your son alive."

I knew Stephen's life had been supernaturally spared. The police, the paramedics, everyone involved at the accident site had commented that he should have died in the crash. The mangled state of our once-shiny white Cavalier spoke to that effect as well. After all, he had been hit by three other vehicles, two of them trucks. Yet he was back to work as a supply teacher in a couple of months, and those who didn't know him well would never have suspected all that he endured, including significant facial reconstruction. That the all-knowing God of heaven, the Omniscient One, would reveal to me that it was the prayers of my father that kept my son alive that blustery winter's day was astounding.

I knew exactly what my Heavenly Father was referring to, for one of my earliest memories involves the prayer times my dad held with my brothers and me whenever my mother, Dorothy West, attended Women's Missionary Prayer Fellowship or other ladies-only events. He would carry us children (eventually there were seven) around the house piggyback-style while he prayed and sang praises to God. Like birds on a wire, we would all sit in a line on our well-worn couch, eagerly anticipating our turn to take flight. Those too young to hop on his back would be cradled in his arms as he wandered from room to room.

Dad began each child's prayer session singing hymns with a gusto he never dared attempt on Sunday morning. Often, he sang,

> What a friend we have in Jesus,
> All our sins and griefs to bare.
> What a privilege to carry,
> Everything to God in prayer."[1]

---

[1] Joseph Scriven, "What a Friend We Have in Jesus" (1855), *Hymns of the Christian Life* (Camp Hill, PA: Christian Publications, 1978), 204.

Even today, I envision those piggyback prayer times when I hear these words, for after singing the hymn my father would engage in a period of passionate supplication. We older ones were forever impacted by the amount of time he spent praying for each and every one of us, and by the intensity of his prayers: for salvation, health and safety, future spouses, future children and grandchildren… What a gift! To be shown the power of my father's prayers and their impact decades after they were earnestly offered up to God! Who knows what blessings could transpire because of our fervent prayers today?

So now, when sleep is elusive, instead of counting sheep into the wee hours, or becoming annoyed and agitated when I awake at three or four in the morning, I pray. First, I thank God for my many blessings. Then I pray for my immediate and extended family. I start with my youngest or oldest sibling and go up or down the list, praying for each of their family members by name. God is truly amazing; often, He will propel a name forward to the top of the list, if that person is in particular need of prayer. I pray for my husband's family as well, the street I live on, the city I live in, the needs of my prayer group, my church, and for whomever or whatever else God brings to mind. Sometimes, if sleep lingers, I simply lie quietly in the stillness of the night, listening Samuel-like (1 Samuel 3:8–10) for the voice of the God who speaks, or, on the most precious of occasions, revelling in the awesome presence and delightful embrace of the Divine.

Keeping the night watch, as I now call it, has lowered my frustration level and seems to have had a positive effect, alleviating my insomnia. Getting fresh air and exercise during the early part of the day, as well as avoiding caffeine, has also helped. Ahh, one of the many benefits of aging—valuable knowledge gleaned from personal experience.

This particular morning (Monday, June 20, 2011) is a little different. I'm arguing with God. Maybe I shouldn't label it arguing when one person is doing all the talking, but in this situation God's silence speaks volumes. Recently, I heard His call to a writing project while attending Write! Canada's spring conference at the Guelph Bible Conference Centre in Guelph, Ontario. The theme of the conference was "Change the World with Words," and now God is about to rock mine.

"Why me?" I ask.

No answer.

"This is a pretty big assignment."

Silence.

"My husband has just retired. And we hope to do some travelling. I don't think he'd want me taking on a big writing project right now."

Again, no response.

"Umm… This is pretty important stuff. I'm… I'm not really that great of a writer."

Not a word.

"It's highly controversial. Don't You think somebody really well-known should tackle this issue… write this book?" I suggest a few potential alternatives.

God finally breaks His silence. "You know Me," He whispers. His voice is soft and gentle, but the words are firm and clear. There's no room for confusion on my part.

I'm silenced by His response. I have no idea why the Sovereign Lord of the universe has revealed His heart to me on this issue, and why He's now asked me to share that heart with you.

Like Moses, I am unqualified (Exodus 4:10–15).

Like the woman at the well, I am unworthy (John 4:4–42).

Like Isaiah, I am undone (Isaiah 6:1–5).

Three small words, "You know Me," yet they comprise the most amazing thing the Holy Spirit has ever communicated to me. I'm honoured and humbled. Joyous—and yes, fearful too, for this assignment is the most important writing project anyone has entrusted me with—ever. This is big! Bigger than scooping third baseman Kelly Gruber, winner of the Gold Glove and Silver Slugger awards for the 1990 Toronto Blue Jays, to be involved in *Home Base,* my first children's novel. Bigger than James Lorimer and Company asking for a sequel to *Shark Attack* and travelling to Japan to research *Sayonara Sharks.* Bigger even than *Brontosaurus Brunch!*

God specializes in the unexpected. I know that; I preach that. Indeed, in God's economy, true life is stranger than fiction. As Christians today, we too should expect the unexpected, to be used of God in astounding ways, for throughout the millennia He has chosen a motley crew to work out His will in this world, to move His Kingdom forward: Sarah, the postmenopausal matron/progenitor of nations (Genesis 17:15–17). Rahab, the prostitute/ancestor of King David *and* Jesus Christ (Joshua 2:1; Matthew 1:5–16). Mary, the virgin/mother of the Messiah (Matthew 1:18–25). Moses, the stuttering shepherd/prince of Egypt (Exodus 4:10; 2:5–10). David, the adulterous murderer/man after God's heart (2 Samuel 11:1–17;1 Samuel 13:14). Paul, the persecuting bully/apostle (Acts 22:1–4; Romans 1:1). Balaam's donkey/prophet (Numbers 22:21–33).

And now me—a writer with many imperfections. Yet if God can use a balking, talking beast of burden, a donkey, to get His message across, I suppose He can use me—a balking, talking, muddled of mind middle-aged woman.

My grace is sufficient for you, for my power is made perfect in weakness. (2 Corinthians 12:9)

I've learned from experience that God blesses those who act in obedience to Him. And so, I begin.

Music speaks what cannot be expressed, soothes the mind and gives it rest, heals the heart and makes it whole, flows from heaven to the soul.

—Anonymous

two

THE THIRD-FOLD

I had put the whole "women and the church" issue to rest several years ago. In fact, God Himself had put it to bed. And turned out the light.

In 1995, Pastor Rick Gay of Peterborough announced an upcoming sermon series highlighting the symbols of the fourfold gospel of the Christian and Missionary Alliance church, originally formulated by Dr. A.B. Simpson, founder of this deeper life movement. I'd grown up in the Cobourg Alliance church, so knew those beloved symbols by heart: Jesus Christ is Saviour, Sanctifier, Healer, and Coming King. As soon as Pastor Rick announced this series, I sensed I would be healed of an old whiplash injury. I can't fully explain the situation; I just knew deep in my spirit I would be healed.

The two years following my car accident were the worst years of my life. An elderly woman had cut me off at the intersection of Mark and Hunter streets, in East City, as I made my way from the Peterborough Centennial Museum to Quaker Oats to pick up my husband after work. Although both vehicles were travelling at a leisurely pace, my little red Chevette was a write-off and immediately hauled away. I was taken to nearby St. Joseph's Hospital by ambulance and released a few hours later. My bumps and bruises and banged-up, bloodied nose healed immediately, but the real trauma began about four weeks after the accident, with arm numbness, headaches, and nausea. Desperately, I searched for healing with numerous trips to doctors, chiropractors, and naturopaths, and I experimented with shiatsu, acupuncture, and finally a pain therapy clinic to help manage my daily life.

I recovered to a point. Outwardly, I seemed fine, and only my closest friends and family knew that I frequently suffered from headaches, couldn't read too much at a time without giving myself a lot of distress, and often felt weak and fatigued. Whenever I took on a major event at Pioneer Clubs, which I co-coordinated during this time, I felt horrible for the next couple of days, beat up, like a soggy dishrag in my grandmother's ancient wringer washing machine. People had prayed for my complete healing a few times, but to no avail. Was there theological significance in the unfolding of A.B. Simpson's fourfold gospel? I now wondered; I hadn't sought healing since totally committing my life to Christ following my father's funeral.

With great anticipation, I awaited the arrival of the healing-themed Sunday. After the sermon, the pastor asked those who would like to be anointed with oil and prayed over to come forward and sit in the front pews. There were quite a few of us—over a dozen, if memory serves me correctly. Confident that I'd be healed, I waited patiently, allowing the other candidates to go ahead of me.

It was three o'clock in the afternoon by the time I blurted out my health concerns to the elders. "My biggest need is complete recovery from whiplash," I stated, explaining a few of the still-lingering symptoms. "And my back is not a hundred percent. It's never been a huge problem, but I do have scoliosis. You know, a crooked spine. I'm sure that's complicated things a bit."

They nodded sympathetically.

"And… and I'm going to get a little greedy with God," I continued. "For some reason, my right arm and hand are really weak right now. In fact, my whole body could use an overhaul."

The elders laughed and placed their hands on my shoulders and neck area while the pastor dabbed a little oil on my forehead. "Dabbed" really isn't the proper word to use here. Pastor Rick had large basketball-playing hands; no doubt we all received an extra-large dollop of that fragrant balm.

These men took turns praying for God's healing power to be released in my body, praying in specifics. One even prayed for something I'd thought about asking for, but never mentioned. Suddenly, I felt a surge of warmth flowing from one man's hand into the right side of my neck. It jerked upright—my neck, that is—startling me a bit, and I knew significant healing had taken place. I wish I'd opened my eyes at the time, taken a peek to see which elder's hand was the conduit for that wonderful, healing warmth, but I kept both closed and simply turned my head from side to side, checking out the extent of my improved mobility.

"My neck is much better," I stated matter-of-factly after the men finished praying. I'd been expecting this divine healing for a few weeks, so wasn't overly excited. That feeling had come with the initial revelation. The elders and pastor, who were probably famished at this point, were no doubt glad I was the last one. We all left the sanctuary without a lot of hoopla.

As well as experiencing increased mobility in my neck, my right hand and arm were strengthened, but only partially. Later in the week, the hand was further restored while I spoke on the phone relating the details of the healing service to a friend. It wasn't until a couple of days later, however, that I fully appreciated the magnitude of my miracle. While merging onto Highway 401 from Highway 115, midway between Cobourg and Oshawa, I glanced over my shoulder, checking for oncoming traffic. Wow! The smoothness with which my neck rotated was incredible. Many years had passed since I'd experienced this wonderful freedom of movement; I'd forgotten what defined normalcy.

"I could have played that part in *The Exorcist*," I jokingly began when I informed Pastor Rick about my improved mobility the next week. "You should have seen my neck spin. And my headaches are gone." I raised my voice, throwing both arms in the air in excitement. "And… and… I can read for hours at a time without it bothering my neck. You've no idea how huge that is. I've always loved to read, ever since I was a little girl."

"I think you should tell the congregation about this," Rick said, grinning from ear to ear, more than pleased the healing service had been productive. "We've got another woman who can tell her story. She's experiencing relief from depression." His countenance grew brighter still and his eyes widened. "Why don't we give a whole morning over to the fact that God can heal body, mind, and spirit?"

Two weeks later, I placed my hands on the beautifully handcrafted walnut pulpit at the front of the Peterborough Christian and Missionary Alliance sanctuary and began my story. Immediately upon contact, I felt a strange surge, almost like electricity, flow into my body through my left hand, streaming up that same arm, then passing through my core and down my right arm, linking me to the pulpit. I'd felt this sensation once before when speaking at my grandmother's funeral at Baltimore United Church. Back then, I'd been startled, hurriedly stepping to the side of the platform, a little dazed and confused. Quickly, I regained my composure, making a joke, then demonstrated at the side of the pulpit how Grandma Buttars used to catch flies. But that's another story.[2]

This time, while speaking at the Peterborough Alliance Church, I immediately recognized the surging sensation that flowed through my body as a sign from God. Both times I experienced this strange phenomenon, I had two hands planted firmly on a pulpit and was speaking in a church. God, I realized, was telling me, "You belong here, speaking for Me."

After concluding my testimony, I made my way back down the aisle and returned to my pew. But God wasn't finished with me yet. My entire body heated up; I felt a sudden shift throughout my spinal region and my right arm strengthened fully. Part of me wanted to jump up and tell everyone what was happening, but the other woman was at the front now, introducing her story, so I kept all this to myself and simply revelled in the wonder of it all. God was showing me His delight, rewarding me for speaking of His goodness and grace.

---

[2] Okay, okay, I'll tell you! She would clap her wrinkled, translucent fingers a few inches above the fly. Startled by the initial movement, the fly would, well, fly and… voila! There it would land, limp and lifeless, in the palm of her hand. I much appreciated her adeptness at this; girls like me, with long, thick hair, found her solution far less troublesome than those golden brown, icky-sticky flypapers that hung, coiled like cobras, from many a farmhouse ceiling.

What's all this got to do with women and the church? Well, much to my surprise, a few months later I felt called to attend Auburn Bible Chapel, a church with Brethren roots. Although things have changed quite a bit over the last couple of decades, at this particular point in time women weren't allowed to speak during Sunday services. They couldn't lead a praise team or a prayer, nor share during Breaking of Bread, the first service. Many kept their heads covered (1 Corinthians 11:1–10), some with hats, others with lacy white head coverings. Though most members of the church were wonderful godly people, the women were excluded from much of church life, unless of course it involved the kitchen, the nursery, the Sunday School, or a women-only event.

What was going on? I thought God had told me I would speak for Him. Needless to say, I was confused. But I learned to love the people (many are friends to this day), and I developed great respect for the value this denomination places on holiness and studying and applying the Word of God. My spiritual life benefited greatly.

At the time, however, I made light of the situation. The Alliance women were working on a missions project, an outreach to the Middle-Eastern world entitled "Lift the Veil." I joked with my closest friends, telling them that I too was on a mission, only mine was to the Brethren world, and it was called "Dump the Doily."

In all seriousness, I was so thankful to God for healing my whiplash that I too would have worn a head covering if I truly believed He wanted me to.

Not without design does God write the music of our lives. Be it ours to learn the tune, and not be dismayed at the "rests." They are not to be slurred over, not to be omitted, not to destroy the melody, not to change the keynote. If we look up, God Himself will beat the time for us. With the eye on Him, we shall strike the next note full and clear.

—John Ruskin, writer and artist

three

THINK OF THE BUTTERFLY

The Eastern Pentecostal Bible College had an incredible library in Peterborough at the time. It was just a short jaunt down the old, abandoned railroad track that bordered the back of our yard on the corner of Benson and Kingan, where I lived with my husband and our three school-aged children. I don't think the people of Peterborough fully appreciated this gem that glittered right in the heart of our city, for it was one of the best theological collections in the country. Forever framed in my mind is the layout of the comfortable lounge area used for perusing periodicals. It's where I was sitting during the shocking events of 9/11.

Unfortunately for us Peterborough residents, the college relocated to Toronto in 2003. I'll also never forget the scholarly value of *The Anchor Bible Dictionary.* The librarians practically pried this beautiful, burgundy six-volume set from my hands in order to load it on the truck that toted the collection to Toronto. I was one of the last people to conduct research at this particular site. Since returning to Peterborough in 2010, the library no longer enjoys the same expansive location, so now, only part of the collection is displayed. Titles can still be accessed from storage, I understand, from what is currently called Master's College and Seminary.

Shortly after landing at Auburn Bible Chapel, I obtained a membership for this library and began carting home armloads of books:

biblical concordances, commentaries on the writings of Paul, and books on the issue of women and the church. The library's colourful stacks offered this bibliophile a rainbow of delight, not only decoratively, but doctrinally as well.

One spring afternoon, I set to work in our sunroom, overlooking the pool and our ever-expanding perennial gardens. With numerous books sprawled over the floral rattan and my Bible in hand, I determined that I would get to the bottom of this; I would ignore the call of the garden and settle the issue of women's role in the church once and for all. I'd majored in history at Trent University, with a minor in psychology, and had always loved the challenge of historical research and debate.

Before I began, I prayed, asking God to share His wisdom with me, telling Him that I was willing to do whatever He wanted, even to the point of remaining silent in the church and wearing a head covering if His word deemed it necessary.

Suddenly, God's spirit pierced my mind. "Why are *you* wasting your time with *this*?" His tone of voice more than captured my attention. It was a sharp reprimand, and to this day it's the only time He's used such a harsh intonation with me.

I listened closely, a little confused.

"I healed you, didn't I?" He reminded, His tone now soft and soothing.

My brow furrowed in bewilderment. And then—it hit me. Of course, He'd further healed me that morning at the Peterborough Christian and Missionary Alliance church, after I publically spoke about the healing of my neck. And it wasn't just women I'd addressed; there were many men in the congregation. Like Pavlov's dog, I made a connection: God wanted me to speak in the church. He'd rewarded me for doing so.

Why did I always feel a need to second-guess myself? The physical sensation I'd experienced when I placed my hands on those pulpits, that was for real. And now, this added confirmation removed any doubt in my mind about God wanting His daughters actively engaged in speaking for Him. A deep sense of peace permeated my inner being. I sensed the Holy Spirit telling me that Paul's instructions regarding the women in the Ephesian church were ephemeral in nature, as opposed to being a directive for all churches for all time (1 Timothy 2:11–12).

What's more, God sounded a little ticked that so many people were wasting their time debating this issue. Did that mean those controversial words of Paul about silence were strictly cultural? Or perhaps situational? No matter. Fuhgeddaboudit! This wasn't something for me to worry about or pursue academically.

Wham! Bam! I slammed those books shut, exalted that my question had been answered by God Himself. I vowed to keep my mouth open whenever the opportunity arose to tell about His amazing goodness. I wouldn't push the women's issue, but if an opportunity presented itself or if someone asked for my opinion, I'd confidently speak up. After refilling my knapsack, I skippity-do-dawed my way back up that old railroad bed, through the arching canopy of trees, past the backside of Trent's Peter Robinson College, across Barnardo Street over to Argyle, then up the hill to the library in order to return those books.

But I continued to read, books from that library and many more—authors such as A.W. Tozer, A.B. Simpson, J.I. Packer, Hannah Whitall Smith, and Evelyn Underhill. I discovered that many of these godly people had been impacted by writers such as Madame Guyon, Francois de Fenelon, as well as many of the Catholic saints. In fact, David Fant's biography of Tozer features an addendum entitled "Dr. Tozer's Recommended Books (for those who would know the deep things of God)." John of the Cross is mentioned there, as is St. Augustine, Thomas à Kempis, Brother Lawrence, Julian of Norwich, and Nicholas of Cusa, among others. These titles contain doctrinal differences from Tozer's own brand of theology, but he felt they would be easily "overbalanced by the spiritual verities" found therein, and he merely presents these books as products of people who "ardently loved their Lord."[3]

As I was new at Auburn Bible Chapel, I hadn't jumped in to volunteer right away. "Not now," God seemed to be saying. I felt compelled to spend the time I'd normally give to church volunteer work reading many of the works these great men and women of God had read. If these works

---

[3] David Fant, *A.W. Tozer: A Twentieth Century Prophet* (Harrisburg, PA: Christian Publications Inc., 1964), 181.

had significantly influenced their spiritual lives, I rationalized, perhaps they would have a positive impact on mine. And with my headaches and neck problems behind me…

All the while, I was helping my daughter with a reading project of her own. As a follow-up assignment to a class trip to Camp Kawartha, an environmental educational facility on Stony Lake, Sarah was to find or build a special outdoor space in her yard or near her home—a nook in which to quietly read and reflect. Together, we hollowed out the inside of a gnarled group of lilacs located in the middle of our yard, making a child's sitting area in the centre of this space with an old, weathered buggy seat. After discovering that the common lilac was one of the recommended shrubs for attracting butterflies, we decided to create a butterfly garden on the south side of the small grove. The trees would provide shelter from the wind, while the southern exposure would offer the necessary warmth and light.

What fun we had: researching, choosing, and planting appropriate plants; adding a small, yellow pedestal-style dish for a "butterfly bath"; then finally, finding the perfect butterfly house, handmade out of recycled barn board. Although we were never sure if any butterflies actually made their home inside, it certainly added charm and character to the garden, and it gave me an emotional satisfaction I couldn't understand at the time. I've since come to realize that the wrinkled, weathered face of this silvery grey shelter reminds me of another wrinkled face, stirring up happy childhood memories of working alongside Grandpa West in his old barn.

I'm sure I did much more reading and reflecting than my daughter. Like a butterfly searching for nectar, I flitted from author to author, saint to saint, drawing from them their passion and love for God, their high regard for stillness before Him.

Be still, and know that I am God; I will be exalted among the nations, I will be exalted in the earth. (Psalm 46:10)

While quietly reading one day, for some reason I became overwhelmingly guilty over the fact that I wasn't visibly busy, that I wasn't doing something publicly constructive for God. *What will people think?* I wondered.

"Think of the butterfly," God immediately responded.

I paused for a moment, mulling over His words. Suddenly, I realized what He'd meant: the butterfly accomplishes its greatest work when it appears to be doing nothing. The guilt took flight. God was telling me that this was okay. This was what He wanted from me at this particular point in my life. A pupa stage—a period of cocooning with my Creator.

This same Creator, however, always beautifully balances times of restoration and renewal, and increased knowledge of Himself, with service to others. It only makes sense that we need to personally experience God's transforming power before we can effectively become His agents of transformation, the resonance of His love and mercy and grace.

Later that year, I was asked to teach the Bible study *Experiencing God: Knowing and Doing the Will of God*, written by Henry Blackaby and Claude King. Unknowingly to me, God had been preparing my heart and mind for this next assignment. I not only used the butterfly as the decor theme for the course, I was able to draw several analogies between the life of the butterfly and that of the Christian: busyness, giving way to stillness and surrender, resulting in astounding transformation.

In addition, many illustrations and quotes from my readings fit seamlessly into the study. From Hannah Whitall Smith's *The Christian's Secret of a Happy Life*:

God has destined us for a higher life than self-life. That just as He has destined the caterpillar to become the butterfly, and therefore has appointed the caterpillar life to die, in order that the butterfly life may take its place, so He has appointed our self-life to die in order that the divine life may become ours instead…

The caterpillar, as it creeps along the ground, must have a widely different "view" of the world around it, from that which the same caterpillar will have when its wings are developed, and it soars in the air above the very places where it crawled.

And similarly the crawling soul must necessarily see things in a very different aspect from the soul that has "mounted up with wings"...

All creatures that have wings can escape from every snare that is set for them, if only they will fly high enough; and the soul that uses its wings can always find a sure "way to escape" from all that can hurt or trouble it. What, then, are these wings? Their secret is contained in the words; "They that wait upon the Lord." The soul that waits upon the Lord is the soul that is entirely surrendered to Him, and that trusts Him perfectly. Therefore we might name our wings the wings of Surrender and of Trust.[4]

This experience, this extended break from the busyness of life, taught me that I could trust God with the smallest details of my life. This same God, the God of Abraham, Isaac, and Jacob, directs the Monarch butterfly on its annual four-thousand-kilometre migration from the fir forests of Central Mexico to the milkweed fields of southern Canada. He directs a common caterpillar to form an elegant green and gold-etched chrysalis, then enables it to burst forth, incredibly arrayed in beauty and grace. He'd been directing, sheltering, nourishing, refreshing, preparing me to mount up with wings.

---

[4] Hannah Whitall Smith, *The Christian's Secret of a Happy Life* (New York, NY: Fleming H. Revell Company, 1916), 240–241.

Trust Me and don't be afraid,
for I am your Strength and Song.
—Sarah Young, author of *Jesus Calling*

four

THE THIRD-FOLD SECRET OF THE HOLY SPIRIT

Out of the blue one day, Mel Gibson phoned. I first met Melanie Gibson through her husband Eugene, when he and I were both working with Peterborough Christian Athletics. Melanie was the children's pastor at Calvary Pentecostal Church, and at one point we attended the same women's Bible study. "I'm preaching this Sunday night at Calvary," she said. "Actually God gave me the message and said it was for you."

"Really?"

"Do you think you can make it?"

"I'll do whatever I can to get there," I said, feeling a bit incredulous that God had spoken specifically about me, yet at the same time intrigued.

I didn't know Melanie that well, but had learned from previous experience that when God speaks it's best to listen up. Her sermon, based on Psalm 78, caused a quickening within me, especially the following verses:

> *He chose David also his servant, and took him from the sheepfolds: From following the ewes great with young he brought him to feed Jacob his people, and Israel his inheritance.* (Psalm 78:70–71, KJV)

The question *"Can God furnish a table in the wilderness?"* (Psalm 78:19, KJV) took on a rhetorical tone, and also resonated. And not merely on a superficial level; these words settled deep in my bones. God would do a work in my life for His Kingdom glory regardless of circumstances. He would work out all the details in His time.

Upon concluding her sermon, Melanie encouraged members of the congregation to come forward for prayer. Avoiding unwanted attention, I remained planted in my pew. Melanie ignored those who had made their way to the front of the church (others moved forward to pray with them), and walked briskly towards me. She placed her hand on my shoulder and prayed with passion and purpose. I don't recall all that she said, but I do remember her praying that God would remove the spirit of fear hampering me from fulfilling *His* purposes.

Two nights later, as I lay in bed in our attic bedroom, I experienced the mysterious moving of the Holy Spirit. The very breath of God seemed to swirl around the room, filling it, then filling me as I breathed in and out—breathing in His presence, His peace, breathing out some of my innermost fears. A wonderful sense of warmth enveloped me and I felt at one with the glorious essence of the eternal, living God. Mere words cannot express the wonder and awe of this moment. Only one comes close: indescribable.

I'd experienced a filling of the Spirit years before, shortly after my father's death, but the physical sensation that accompanied it had been water-related. While praying on the living room couch one day, surrendering my will to God's alone, a warm liquid seemed to fill my body, from the tips of my toes to the top of my head.

I will sprinkle clean water on you, and you will be clean; I will cleanse you from all your impurities and from all your idols. I will give you a new heart and put a new spirit in you; I will remove from you your heart of stone and give you a heart of flesh. And I will put my Spirit in you and move you to follow my decrees and be careful to keep my laws. (Ezekiel 36:25–27)

For a couple of years, a purification of my human spirit took place through this spiritual washing by the Holy Spirit. A fountain of joy bubbled within, and with it came new boldness for Jesus. At the time, however, I made the mistake of assuming a one-time surrender, and subsequent filling, was the ultimate achievement in the Christian life—kind of like expecting an oil change to last the lifetime of a car. As time progressed, I realized something was amiss, for I totally lost the manifestation of the Spirit's presence, as well as my boldness and joy. I was taking God for granted, neglecting Bible study and prayer; He withdrew His physical manifestation, causing me to hunger and thirst for Him all the more.

Desperately, I searched for answers, reading everything I could find about the Holy Spirit. Eventually, at a used book sale in the foyer of Ferndale Bible Church, where our young family attended at the time, I discovered a little green booklet entitled *The Three-Fold Secret of the Holy Spirit.*[5] Recently culled from their library, this dilapidated copy offered the most intelligent, balanced material I've read concerning the Holy Spirit. It proved to be the best ten cents I've ever spent, for upon reading this tiny volume, authored by James H. McConkey, I experienced an incredible spiritual awakening. Initial surrender to God was only the beginning, I discovered; I needed to live a life of surrender. Up to this point, I'd learned the first and second secret of the Holy Spirit: the Incoming (upon salvation) and the Infilling (upon my recent surrender and consecration). But I hadn't yet understood the third—Abiding in Christ. Being filled with the Spirit was one thing; walking by the Spirit was quite another. Sanctification was not so much a state to attain as it was a Person to know and build a relationship with. I needed to drink daily from Jesus' fountain of living water, so like the woman at the well (John 4:10–14), I too needed never thirst again. This realization would mark my life indelibly. The cost? Only a dime!

The Bible says, *"Walk by the Spirit and you will not carry out the desires of the flesh"* (Galatians 5:16, NASB). You'll also learn that the Christian life is one grand adventure just waiting to unfold— a lifelong

---

[5] James H. McConkey, *The Three-Fold Secret of the Holy Spirit* (Pittsburgh, PA: Silver Publishing Society, 1897).

journey of personal discovery and spiritual growth. It's not always easy, but it's never boring.

This time around, after Melanie Gibson's sermon at Calvary Pentecostal Church and the midnight meeting with my Maker, I vowed to abide in Christ. I would continually immerse myself in His Word and spend time with Him in praise and prayer. Eventually, through the influence of the authors mentioned earlier and my study of the Bible, I developed a strong consciousness of God's presence and love, and an attitude of praise and prayer began to permeate my life—a realization of what the apostle Paul meant when he encouraged us to *pray without ceasing"* (1 Thessalonians 5:17, KJV).

A gaze heavenward,
A beholding in order to become,
A practice of the presence of God.
A continual linking to the vine,
A resting in Jesus, drawing upon His power and strength.

The more I aligned my heart with God and His Son, the greater my experience of the guidance, wisdom, and power of the Holy Spirit. The more I sought the life and work of the Spirit, the greater my desire to obey the Father and glorify the Son. One of the keys to unlocking increased intimacy with the Triune God, I discovered, was developing relationship with all three persons of the Trinity.

A few words of caution are in order here: there is no one formula for knowing God intimately, for experiencing the deeper Christian life. Our Abba Father, our Creator, possesses the ultimate in creativity, interacting with each and every one of His children according to His Kingdom purposes, gifting each of us a unique spiritual history. Even so, we're all in process, we're all on a path (often one with many bumps and bends) as we learn to *act justly* and *love mercy* and *walk humbly* with our God (Micah 6:8). Walking humbly is key, allowing us to walk hand in hand. According to Elizabeth Sherrill, master ghostwriter of many bestselling Christian books,

The longer the walk, the more our individuality emerges… For God, who doesn't make duplicates even of snowflakes, is filling his heaven with millions upon millions of unique creations.[6]

But back to the point of this book. The fruit of Melanie Gibson's preaching and prayer was evident in my life, further confirming that God didn't want His daughters silent in the church. The subsequent "breath of God" experience, I would later discover, was of particular significance. In Hebrew, "breath" denotes creativity. According to Victor Shepherd, Professor of Systematic and Historical Theology at Tyndale and Adjunct Professor of Theology at the University of Toronto,

The breath of God that God breathes into his own people is that movement of God upon us and within us which enlivens our creativity and frees it for service in God's kingdom… Where the Spirit is concerned, creativity has nothing to do with extraordinary artistic talent. The creativity of the Spirit, rather, is simply the freeing, the freeing up, the magnification and multiplied usefulness of *any* gift we have in order that this talent might now be [used] for God's purposes…[7]

Several years of active ministry at Auburn Bible Chapel followed: coordinating Pioneer Clubs, leading Bible studies, speaking at women's events, then becoming the head of women's ministry. At the same time, God was wonderfully creative, providing ample opportunity for me to speak to mixed audiences on His behalf: seniors and community groups, funeral eulogies, even supply preaching on occasion. I also completed a few Master's courses through Tyndale Seminary in Toronto by enrolling in their long-distance education program.

And all the while, I wrote. Before coming to Auburn, it was children's books, but now I felt compelled to produce Christian material: a children's

---

[6] Elizabeth Sherrill, *All the Way to Heaven* (Grand Rapids, MI: Fleming H. Revell, 2002), 144–145.

[7] Victor Shepherd, "The Holy Spirit as Breath, Oil, Dove and Fire," Accessed: September 8, 2014 (http://victorshepherd.ipage.com/Sermons/the_holy_spirit_as_breath.htm).

Christmas musical on the theme of abiding in Christ, an Old Testament allegory entitled *Guardian of the Lamp*, an accompanying Bible study on understanding the Old Testament, personal experience stories for Gospel Publishing House in Missouri, and anthology contributions to *Chicken Soup for the Soul* and *A Second Cup of Hot Apple Cider*. In fact, I was pretty content with my homemaker/writer/speaker/retiree life when God decided to assign me this major writing project, and so the argument that fateful morning upon returning from my second Write! Canada conference.

Why now, I wondered, *this direction to write about women and the church?*

The music comes from the fiddler's heart,
through his strings… straight into your heart.
—Father John Angus Rankin, Cape Breton musician

five

THE GEBIRA

It all began with the *gebira*. The *gebira* of ancient Judah was the one who set in motion an unexpected journey deep into the heart of God where He amazingly revealed His extreme love and compassion for His daughters, and His heartbreak over the way the church treats the women He created in His image.

So God created man in his own image, in the image of God he created him; male and female he created them. (Genesis 1:27)

While researching the story of Queen Athaliah for an Old Testament Bible study to accompany *Guardian of the Lamp*, I ran into this Hebrew word for the first time. The Old Testament has four Hebrew words that are translated "queen" in English. One of them is *gebira,* and this word is used to refer to Athaliah (2 Kings 10:13). *Gebira* is the feminine form of *gebir*, meaning "lord" or "master." I discovered references to the male *gebir* in my theological word books, but found it more difficult to access the *gebira*. Apparently, in the southern kingdom of Judah, the *gebira* played an important role, wielding considerable power and influence. *The Anchor Bible Dictionary* attests to this fact:

As Queen Mother, Athaliah now held the exalted position of "sovereign" (Heb. Gebira), which included an extraordinary ceremonial position, and probably also special influences on matters of state.[8]

It's significant that the mothers of the Davidic kings are listed in the Old Testament, and it's not merely because of their maternal function. The Queen Mother was often the king's chief advisor—his lady counsellor. As far as Athaliah's son, King Ahaziah, is concerned, *"He too walked in the ways of the house of Ahab, for his mother encouraged him in doing wrong"* (2 Chronicles 22:3). Upon the death of her son, Queen Athaliah didn't want to lose her throne or crown, not to mention the considerable power which came with the position of *gebira*, evident in the following verse:

> *Say to the king and to the queen mother, "Come down from your thrones, for your glorious crowns will fall from your heads."* (Jeremiah 13:18)

Many people consider the infamous Jezebel to be the wickedest woman in the Bible, the baddest bad girl of the bunch, but I believe Athaliah should wear that crown. In order to secure her regal position, she attempted to destroy the entire royal family, which included assassinating her own grandchildren. Although she successfully seized the throne, becoming queen of Judah for six years, Jehosheba, a sister of King Ahaziah, bravely hid one of Athaliah's grandsons, saving him from the slaughter. Six years later, Joash, descendent of David and forefather of Jesus Christ, was brought out of hiding and anointed king. The courage of Jehosheba saved one small baby, and in so doing allowed another small baby to save us all!

And what of evil Athaliah? Well, she was unceremoniously slain with the sword as she approached the Horse Gate of the palace grounds (2 Chronicles 23:15). Understanding the position of the *gebira* helps us not condone, but more readily relate to her desperate, egotistical actions.

Upon discovering this information, I wondered if it might be too feminist for my Bible study. Although significant change had taken

---

[8] David Noel Freedman, ed. *The Anchor Bible Dictionary, Volume One* (New York, NY: Doubleday, 1992), 512.

place at Auburn Bible Chapel over the years (women could now lead praise and worship, and share verbally during communion), this was still a church with Brethren roots. I appreciated the fact that our women loved to study God's Word (the name of our group is Women in the Word), but would people feel I was promoting a hidden agenda by drawing attention to this advisory position of women? Would they think I was seeking power or trying to stir up trouble? I'd pretty much decided to leave out the information regarding the *gebira,* but then, as with everything else I included in the study, I sought God's will on the matter. Dropping to my knees, I prayed, "God, I'm not going to include this *gebira* stuff, but if for some reason you want me to, just… just let me know."

Five seconds later, as I walked past the tightly crammed bookshelves of our Weller Street home, a cobalt blue spine emblazoned with bright gold and white lettering seemed to call out to me. I'd purchased this particular book at a garage sale years before, along with several other titles, but hadn't yet read it. As the book summoned from the middle of the shelf, the Holy Spirit whispered, "There is something for you here."

I rescued Tony Campolo's *Wake Up America! Answering God's Radical Call While Living in the Real World* from bookshelf oblivion. It fell open to page 103. Halfway down the page, a subtitle in bold-faced print startled me: **Women as Oppressed Christians.** I continued to read.

> We need not go to minority groups like the African-American community to find a people with whom a prophet can identify. There is a group of oppressed people within the mainstream of American Christianity that is beginning to rise up in righteous indignation against the church and against society. I am referring to women.[9]

As a general rule, I wouldn't encourage anyone, Christian or otherwise, to randomly open a book and claim the first passage they read is from God, but this was definitely a supernatural situation: the book beckoned,

---

[9] Tony Campolo, *Wake Up America! Answering God's Radical Call While Living in the Real World* (New York, NY: Harper Collins Publishers, 1991), 103.

the Spirit spoke, and the page presented addressed the exact situation I'd recently prayed about. Furthermore, I'd learned long ago to pay particular attention to what happens immediately after one prays. And then to ask God for confirmation in the following days, which in this case I did receive.

I scanned a few more pages, then read the chapter's concluding paragraph.

> What women will gain in their struggle for cultural liberation will not only bless them—it will bless all of us male chauvinists who have given them such a hard time and called them degrading names. It just may be that the revival that the church needs if it is to challenge the psychic slavery and deadness of America will come from women. The prophet who delivers us from our consumer-oriented mind-set could well be a prophetess.[10]

I'd heard some incredible stories about men degrading women speakers. One of the most horrific is this account, shared by Anne Graham Lotz in the *Washington Post*:

> What legitimate, Biblical role do women have within the church? That question demanded an answer early in my ministry when I accepted an invitation to address a large convention of pastors. When I stood in the lectern at the convention center, many of the 800 church leaders present turned their chairs around and put their backs to me. When I concluded my message I was shaking. I was hurt and surprised that godly men would find what I was doing so offensive that they would stage such a demonstration, especially when I was an invited guest. And I was confused. Had I stepped out of the Biblical role for a woman? While all agree that women are free to help in the kitchen, or in the nursery, or in a secretary's chair, is it unacceptable for a woman to take a leadership or teaching position?[11]

---

[10] Ibid, 106.

[11] Cheryl Schatz, "Ann Graham Lotz and 800 pastors' shame," *Women in Ministry*, October 24, 2008 (http://strivetoenter.com/wim/2008/10/24/anne-graham-lotz-and-800-pastors-shame/). Quoting Anne Graham Lotz, from the *Washington Post*.

One thing I do know: Jesus would never have treated Anne Graham Lotz in such a demeaning manner. His example, found in the four gospel accounts of His life, reflects the exact opposite.

He engages (John 4:4–42).
He encourages (Luke 10:38–42).
He edifies (Mark 5:25–34; John 8:1–11).
He educates (Luke 10:38–42).
He elevates (Luke 10:38–42; 13:10–16).
He enlists (Matthew 28:1–10; John 4:4–42).

Jesus, in fact, goes out of His way to break the traditions of the religious elite. One of the best examples of this is His interaction with the woman at the well in Samaria (John 4:4–42). Travelling north from Judea to Galilee, Jesus and His disciples took a shortcut through Samaria, stopping at Jacob's Well, the limestone cistern in the shadow of Gerizim, the Samaritan's holy mountain. Tired and thirsty, Jesus rested by the well of the famous patriarch while his disciples headed into the nearby town of Sychar in order to buy food. Around six o'clock in the evening, Jesus engaged our Samaritan sister, uttering six small words that trampled the religious traditions of the time: *"Will you give me a drink?"* (John 4:7).

First of all, Jesus publically addressed a woman. The fact that she was immoral is mute; any conversation with any woman, no matter how lofty, would have gone against propriety. Talking with a woman could lead to adultery. And to continue the conversation past the initial request for a drink? Why would He, a learned rabbi, bother? Women were considered incapable of intellectual dialogue or spiritual debate.

Secondly, she was a Samaritan, a woman of mixed race. In 722 BC, after the barbaric Assyrian army destroyed the northern state of Israel, the tribes were dispersed, exported, creating what has become known as the ten lost tribes of Israel. Foreigners, other victims of Assyrian aggression, were imported, herded like cattle into Samaria, the capital of the north. The Assyrians knew that the best way to destroy a nation was to dismantle their culture and religion. This mixture of people became known as the Samaritans, and they were always considered outsiders and inferiors by the Judeans to the south, even after the Babylonian exile (Ezra 4:1–3). On their way to Galilee, many Jewish people would walk through Perea, east of the Jordan (several days out of their way), in order to avoid these people of mixed religion and race.

Finally, Jesus asked the Samaritan woman for a drink of water, despite the fact that accepting a cup or jar, or any vessel, from her hands would make Him ceremonially unclean. There were stringent rules regarding what a Jew, let alone a Jewish rabbi, could and could not touch. During menstruation,

> women were considered *niddah,* and were to be avoided by men lest they become contaminated. Rabbinic expositions on *niddah* classify Samaritan woman as *niddah* from the day of their birth (mNidd. 4:1; mNidd. 5:1)![12]

Jesus' actions defied ritual law in unthinkable ways.

This account in the gospel of John is beyond significant. It not only records Jesus' biggest one-on-one conversation with anyone in the Bible, regardless of gender, it confirmed that Jesus' mission was to be the Saviour of the entire world, not just the Jewish people. The Samaritan woman could meet His physical need, His thirst for water, but Jesus could offer something far greater.

If you knew the gift of God and who it is that asks you for a drink, you would have asked him and he would have given you living water. (John 4:10)

How the words "living water" would have arrested her attention. Not to mention Jesus' use of the word "gift." The Greek word used here, *dorea,* signifies a particular type of gift—a free gift, a gift without need of repayment, a gift highlighting the beneficent nature of the Giver. "It

---

[12] Sue and Larry Richards, *Every Woman in the Bible* (Nashville, TN: Thomas Nelson Publishers, 1999), 160.

38

is always used in the NT of a spiritual or supernatural gift."[13] Why, if she had access to "living water," no longer would she need to make the daily trek to Jacob's Well, nor the more arduous return, laden with her heavy vessel. This woman was about to discover, however, that she was the earthen vessel in need of water, water that is heaven sent.

"Living water" signifies running water, such as that flowing from a stream or river, as opposed to still, stagnant water found languishing in a pool or pond. "Living water" is life-giving and safe to drink, while stagnant water promotes sickness and disease, in some cases death. Only "living water" was utilized in certain cleansing rituals in Judaism to purify someone who was unclean. Jesus was making a bold statement here, declaring that He alone could cleanse her of her sin.

Jesus' mission was more important than the "sin" of multiplying words with a woman. Each word He spoke brought her closer to faith, until she eventually trusted that He was, indeed, the Messiah. In the process, He affirmed her worth, offering love and acceptance, despite her gender, despite her past, despite cultural parameters, elevating and liberating women in a manner unheard of in first-century Palestine. The woman at the well no longer needed to put her faith in the broken cisterns the world had to offer (John 4:18), *"broken cisterns that cannot hold water"* (Jeremiah 2:13); she experienced a life-changing, life-giving encounter with the ultimate spring of "living water," the source of abundant life in the here and now, and eternal life in the hereafter.

In turn, this redeemed woman evangelized her fellow Samaritans, proclaiming the "good news," the gospel.

Many of the Samaritans from that town believed in him because of the woman's testimony. (John 4:39)

This is, by the way, the same "good news," the same "living water," that Anne Graham Lotz was promoting at the convention of pastors.

---

[13] W.E. Vine, *Vine's Complete Expository Dictionary of Old and New Testament Words* (Nashville, TN: Thomas Nelson Publishing, 1996), 264.

How beautiful on the mountains are the feet of those who bring good news, who proclaim peace, who bring good tidings, who proclaim salvation… (Isaiah 52:7)

My hope and prayer is that all of God's children, both men and women, become eternal springs, Christ-like conduits of this life-giving flow.

The phrase "Women as Oppressed Christians" found midway down that page of *Wake Up America!* and highlighted in bold-faced print, emboldened me. I need not worry about mentioning the *gebira* in my Bible study. This was pretty tame stuff compared to Tony Campola's writing. Pretty tame stuff compared to the words and actions of Jesus Christ, as recorded in Holy Writ. What's more, the dust jacket of Campola's book delivered prophetic words of wisdom: "In *Wake Up America!* you will capture a new vision, a new purpose for your own life."

How pleased I was to meet Tony shortly after this introduction to his literary work, at a Church in the City event.[14] Tony signed my copy of the book while I explained how God had used his words to powerfully speak to me.

Glenn and Sheila Duncan also recommended a book to me at this time—*Community 101, Reclaiming the Local Church as Community of Oneness*, authored by Gilbert Bilezikian, professor emeritus of biblical studies at Wheaton College. This book is more about building authentic community than tackling the women's issue, but Bilezikian believes this is part of the same predicted change from old covenant to new community that took place with the advent of Christ. One of the founders of Willow Creek Community Church, Bilezikian presents views much different than those I'd been exposed to:

> Church leaders who, without justification, interfere with God's plan by excluding any of their members from full participation in gifts-based ministries take upon themselves a frightful responsibility. They prohibit Christians from fulfilling their

---

[14] A relational network of evangelical churches and Christian ministries in Peterborough, Ontario.

God-assigned calling. Worse yet, they deprive the kingdom of the powerful potential invested in the church by its Lord for its growth and outreach. Should it appear that a hermeneutical choice needs to be made between disobeying Scripture by opening ministry to all or disobeying Scripture by restricting ministry to some, it is obvious which form of disobedience would be less detrimental to the church... If error there is, it is better to stray helping the kingdom than cheating it.[15]

I was incredulous that so many well-respected Christians felt this way. Even more so by the fact that God was this concerned about the way the church treats women, even to the point of labelling it oppression. After all, this couldn't begin to compare with the oppression that many women, especially those in Middle-Eastern countries, face on a daily basis, or with the slavery inflicted upon young women by the exploitive sex trade that runs rampant throughout the world. What should I do (could I do) with this information God sent me through the pages of Tony Campolo's book? With the fact that Christian women in North America were oppressed?

---

[15] Gilbert Bilezikian, *Community 101: Reclaiming the Local Church as Community of Oneness* (Grand Rapids, MI: Zondervan Publishing House, 1997), 82.

It takes more skill than I can tell
To play the second fiddle well.
—C.H. Spurgeon, Prince of Preachers

six

THE POWER OF STORY

That spring, I felt compelled to attend my first Write! Canada—The Word Guild's three-day annual writer's conference held each June in Guelph, Ontario. It was wonderful to mix and mingle with like-minded writers and speakers. The spirit of community and oneness Bilezikian speaks of in his book was evident on the grounds that weekend, especially in the worship sessions. Despite diverse denominational backgrounds and a wide disparity in areas of interest and domains of influence, we were united in common purpose—glorifying our God.

In order to keep the price of the conference within my budgetary constraints, I shared a cabin with several women. We all shared a love of words, a love of God's Word, and most importantly, a love of the Living Word. Sleeping in an upper bunk made me feel like a kid again, reminding me of wonderful summer weeks spent at Camp Glen Witmoc, located over the bridge, through the woods, and up the hill from Glen Rocks Bible Conference on the shores of Lake Rousseau, in Ontario's beautiful, rugged Muskoka region. Here in Guelph, however, I had to contend with something no young Witmoc camper ever inflicted upon me: everyone in my cabin snored, one woman particularly loud (you know who you are).

Despite the lack of sleep, the conference proved amazing. And God became Jehovah-Rapha on my behalf—the Lord who heals (Exodus 15:25–26)—physically restoring my body the final morning, enabling me to carry on that closing day, refreshed and alert. The food was pretty amazing too. Much better than my camp days, I have to admit (except, of course, when Gwen Bickle was the cook). What really fed my heart and soul, however, and provided ample food for thought, was Brian Stiller's plenary speech on the Friday night. Humorous, informative, inspiring, it encouraged me greatly. But none of that mattered. Our Creator God spoke through him and through the power of story in order to creatively communicate with me.

Dr. Stiller was introduced by award-winning writer, editor, and speaker Wendy Nelles, co-founder of The Word Guild and Director Emerita of Write! Canada. She referred us to the internet in order to glean information regarding his many accomplishments and access his curriculum vitae, choosing instead to relate more personal experiences. Apparently, Brian was the first person she knew who used the terminology "paradigm shift," a concept which became popular in the 1980s. She recalled a series of lectures he gave related to

> understanding our times, and informing and educating Christians so they could more effectively understand contemporary culture and more importantly—engage, not retreat.[16]

Stiller's entire presentation was engaging, especially his captivating conclusion. Seconds before he began the following narrative, I quietly prayed, asking God to let me know if I should keep the encounter with Campola's book to myself or speak of it publicly, maybe even write about it. Perhaps the concept of understanding our times, coupled with Stiller's encouragement to document our personal stories, triggered this sidebar of thought. Or maybe it was the simple fact that I'm a little ADD and my brain likes to go on a bit of a walkabout from time to time. Regardless, I was pulled from my own ponderings when Stiller announced, "Let me tell you a story."

Unfortunately, the printed page doesn't do justice to his story, for his friendly countenance warmed the entire auditorium, his eyes sparkled,

---

[16] Wendy Nelles, *Write! Canada, Plenary 2,* 2009, compact disc.

his voice enthralled, bringing just the right tempo and emotion to the telling, sweeping us all to another time, another place...

There are three GIs. Second World War. These guys had lived their lives together in a small mid-western U.S. town. Their parents were friends. They were in the same cub pack, same baseball team. Through high school. Through college.

They're in the Second World War in the Italian theatre. It's late afternoon. They're working together in the same squadron and unbeknownst to them there's a sniper. And he cuts down one of the three and he dies.

The other two... have no time to be shocked.

They'd better do something. And so one says, "We've got to bury our buddy. Where do we bury him?"

And the other one said, "Well, I saw a little cemetery back across the hill behind a little church."

And so, running low to the ground, they carried their buddy.

Sure enough, here was this little Catholic church, and in the back, this little cemetery.

Making sure there was no one watching, they took out their collapsible shovels and began to dig. And as soon as they did, they heard a noise and they saw a priest running from the church waving his arms.

And before the GIs could give a word, this priest, in his faltering English, said, "Are you Catholic?"

And they said, "No, we're Protestant."

And the father said, "No, you... you can't bury here."

The GI said, "Well, this is our friend. He's died. Where can we bury him?"

The Father thought for a moment. "Guys, come with me." So they walked around the fence and he said, "You can bury him here."

So they did...

It's early in the morning before sun's up. And one of them wakes up. Now grief... is rolling in. And he wakes his buddy and says, "You know, we never really gave a farewell to our buddy. Let's go back."

So they slipped on their clothes and before the sun broke they got back to the cemetery. And they couldn't find the grave. It was gone!

And, they're just... they're saying, "Yeah... yeah... It was here."

They heard the door close and there was the same priest. He was getting up for early morning mass, and he came running down and before he had a chance to say anything one of the GI's said, "Father, where's the grave?"

And the Father, in his broken English, said, "Oh... I went home last night. It was so wrong! It was so wrong! So this morning, I got up early, and I moved the fence.[17]

Stiller continued, "You know, as writers we are fence movers. We open the opportunity for others to experience grace and love... and newness, and be transformed."

As Stiller uttered the words "fence movers," I had an overwhelming feeling that God had just answered my prayer. I was being called to move a fence, and I had a pretty good idea which one it was. Although I didn't fully understand as yet all that would be involved, I knew one tool I would utilize: my pen. "Writers," Stiller had said, "are agents of transformation."

Suddenly, with no warning, I began to weep. No matter how hard I tried, I couldn't dam the deluge. What was *this* about? A little embarrassed by what was happening, I quickly wiped away the evidence and slumped in my seat, hoping to make myself as invisible as possible. I was near the back of the auditorium on the far end of a row, sitting beside Beverly Helmond, the friend from church I'd driven to the conference. Thankfully, she's much taller than I am and few people noticed the tears.

Just for the record, I like to be in control of my emotions and do not readily cry in public. Maybe just a little at a wedding, baptism, funeral, chick flick, or significant sporting event, now that I'm postmenopausal,

---

[17] Dr. Brian Stiller, *Write! Canada, Plenary 2*, 2009, compact disc.

but this was at an earlier point in my life. I grew up with six brothers, in the countryside near Baltimore, Ontario and we played rough and tumble: green apple fights and barnyard baseball in the summers, pond hockey in the winter, and tag-team wrestling all year long on the double bed in the backroom. I've been chased home from school by boys swinging snakes at my head, and yes, after walking miles there in the first place, sometimes in sub-zero weather—uphill both ways.[18] I do not cry over spilt milk, lost jewellery, or flooded basements, and being a farm girl whose grandfather regularly drowned unwanted kittens in a brown burlap feed sack, not even the death of a beloved pet.

The point is—these were uncommon tears! Granted, in this story about being an outsider, there might have been a small element of what Barbara Tuchman, Pulitzer-Prize-winning historian, calls a distant mirror effect: true stories that reflect our own experiences. I'll admit that as a woman in the church, many times I've felt left out, forced outside the fence, excluded (buried even), simply because of gender. But I'd learned to accept it. Believe me, I would never cry about it. I sensed for the most part that this torrent of tears was a mysterious moving of the Holy Spirit, as God's presence was thick in that auditorium. What was He up to? The Spirit-filled life was proving to be a wild, unpredictable adventure. What would happen next?

---

[18] This is not a feeble attempt at a joke, by the way, but swear-on-the-Bible truth.

If a feller can't bow he'll never make a fiddler. He might make a violin player, but he'll never make a fiddler. It's all in the rhythm of the bow.

—Tommy Jarrell, American fiddler

seven

WOMEN IN MINISTRY

Shortly after the conference, I awoke one morning with the words "Go see Karl House" impressed upon my mind. A few years earlier, someone had given me a set of his sermon tapes on the work of the Holy Spirit. I could ask him about this bewildering burst of emotion, I decided. It wasn't as if I was a total stranger; I'd conducted a little research on *Guardian of the Lamp* at his church library before the Living Hope offices moved from downtown Peterborough to their more expansive Lansdowne Street East location. I would take him a copy of my new novel.

When I arrived at Living Hope that Friday morning, I found Karl standing in a bright, open area located in the middle of the church complex—their fellowship room, I would later discover. I related what had happened with Campola's book, Stiller's story, and the subsequent weepfest.

He smiled, nodding his head understandingly. "The Holy Spirit was weeping through you," he explained. "He's grieved by the church's treatment of women."

Karl was moving to the Tampa Bay area, in Florida. "To begin a new work," he said. In fact, this was his last day at Living Hope. "But I've got something for you," he added, smiling broadly before his tall, lean frame strode purposefully toward the adjacent hallway.

Quickly, I followed along, not wanting to take up valuable time on what would no doubt be a busy day.

"I'm going to print you off a copy," he called over his shoulder, disappearing through the first doorway on the left.

Karl's office was empty, swept clean, except for one stapled stack of papers lying face-up in the centre of the large wooden table which dominated the middle of the room, and one cardboard box, perched rather precariously on the corner of his desk. As I glanced at the title on that packet, "Women in Ministry," my eyes grew bright and my mouth dropped open.

"This is a bit bizarre," I said. "Don't you think? It's as if this was just sitting here waiting for me."

We both agreed that this was more than mere coincidence.

Karl photocopied his sermon notes so I could take a copy home. Apparently, this issue was something he was working through, and now he has kindly granted permission for me to share this information with you:

Women in Ministry:
Reflections for Consideration
Living Hope Christian Reformed Church
Pastor Karl House
March 1999, Revised January 2004

GENESIS 1:26–28 AND GENESIS 5:1–2
Both men and women bear the image of God. Both men and women are commissioned to exercise stewardship over creation. Is there a suggestion of male predominance here?

GENESIS 2:20B–25
Traditionally, the word "helper" has been interpreted to suggest that Eve was subordinate to Adam. But, who is the one in need of help here—Adam or Eve? It was Adam. And what did he need help with? The dishes? No. The only reason given in the text is that Adam needed help with not being alone. So Eve was created not as domestic help for Adam, but as one who would mutually share with him the responsibility of carrying out God's commission for human life, namely, to *be fruitful*

and increase in number; fill the earth and subdue it."Which, by the way, is pretty hard to do all alone!

Also in regards to being a "helper," it's important to note that God is often called our helper throughout Scripture (See Exodus 18:4; Deuteronomy 33:7, 26, 29; Psalm 33:20, etc.) Certainly that doesn't make God inferior to us! In fact, the Hebrew language has four other words for "helper" that denote subordination. None of these words are used in reference to women in Genesis 2.

Finally, Adam's first reaction to the creation of Eve is an exclamation of equality, mutuality, complementarity. None of the animals fit the bill. They couldn't fill Adam's God-created need for another human being. But Eve did. She was a perfect fit. And once again, in no way does Adam's reaction denote male superiority and female inferiority. In effect, he says, *"Finally, I found another me [bone of my bones and flesh of my flesh]… a her!"*

Much of what we automatically consider promoting male predominance in the creation accounts is more likely read back from our understandings of 1 Corinthians 11 and Timothy 2. But are we reading too much male predominance into these New Testament passages, and therefore, back into creation? We'll come to these passages later.

GENESIS 3:1–6

Why did Satan target Eve? Was it because she was morally inferior to Adam? There is no suggestion of this in the text. Rather the narrative tells us that Adam received the command to not eat of the tree firsthand from God, which suggests that Eve got it secondhand from Adam. Could it be, then, that Satan targeted Eve because her secondhand knowledge would make her easier to deceive? In fact, it seems that her knowledge of God's command was faulty considering she added that they weren't supposed to even touch the fruit. Obviously, she lacked details about the command. And whose fault was that—Eve's or Adam's?

And where was Adam through all of this? He seems to be with her, maybe right at her side. Certainly, he could have stopped her from eating the fruit, but no such action is mentioned. Therefore, Adam is as responsible for the Fall as Eve. In fact, the Bible labels Him as the one who brought sin and death into the world. Eve was simply deceived. Once again, does this have to do with moral inferiority inherent to Eve's make-up or the fact that Adam was told directly by God to not eat of the tree, and therefore, held more responsible?

GENESIS 3:16

Male domination is finally explicitly mentioned. And it's one of the consequences of the Fall. It's a curse, not a blessing!

JUDGES 4

Deborah is often said to be the female exception that proves the male leadership rule. But read the text again for the first time. There is no suggestion from the text that judgeship was reserved for men only and that she was an exception. She may have been exceptional, but not necessarily an exception. The fact that Barak was commissioned by God (through Deborah) does not take away from the fact that she was considered the prophet and the judge. Just consider the prophecy itself. In no way does the prophecy call for Barak to replace Deborah as judge and prophet—a male replacing a female. Rather, the prophecy calls for a division of labour: Deborah being the judge and prophet, Barak being the general of the army. In fact, to be technical, Deborah sent for Barak. Certainly this suggests that her position was one of greater authority than his own.

Regarding Deborah's prophecy that a woman would receive the honour for defeating Sisera, this prophecy wasn't fulfilled necessarily by Deborah herself, but by Jael (see Judges 5:24–27). So once again, this wasn't Deborah's way of trying to get a man to do a man's job by hook or by crook, but simply stating the consequences when unbelief prevents us from doing what God has told us to do. We miss out on the blessing that God intends for us because of our fear.

Also note that Deborah was married. If male leadership in Scripture is one of male superiority, then what does this example say about the supposed automatic transference of male headship in marriage to male headship in terms of leadership among God's people corporately? In other words, does headship at home necessarily mean headship in the church? And what does headship mean? Stay tuned.

2 KINGS 22:11–20
Prophetess Huldah, the wife of Shallum, was officially consulted by a delegation from King Josiah. Was she consulted simply because there weren't any men prophets around? According to biblical history, Jeremiah and Zephaniah were prophets at that time.

MATTHEW 20:20–28
What is the nature of leadership in Christ's "upside-down" Kingdom? Service! In fact, Jesus our Head got down on His knees to wash the disciples' feet and spread out His hands to die in our place.

ACTS 2:17–18
In the New Covenant the ministry of prophesy is opened up even further than the Old. In the Old Covenant spiritually anointed men and women were prophets. In the New Covenant all of God's people, including both men and women, are anointed to be prophets.

ROMANS 12:3–8 AND 1 CORINTHIANS 12
The passages on spiritual gifts are not gender specific. The sense one gets is that Paul didn't think certain gifts were intended for men only.

1 CORINTHIANS 11:2–16
Traditionally, this passage has been used to point out that Paul sets up a clear chain of command—from God to Jesus, from Jesus to man, and from man to woman. Therefore, women are subordinate to men, both in the church and in the home.

But this is a confusing passage and much has been written to try to figure it out. At this point I can't reconstruct exactly what Paul is reacting against and what Paul is saying. But let me make a few comments that may be helpful.

The overarching subject here is the protocol of men and women in worship and not necessarily the relationship between men and women in general.

Whatever the passage is saying, it clearly states that both men and women are to pray and prophesy in church.

There are many meanings for the word "head." The first is the literal meaning of the word, namely, your head. The second is that of source or origin. We use the word still today in this sense when we talk about the head of a river or the source of a river. There are two other meanings to the Greek word head which were used very infrequently. One was a technical meaning referring to a ruler of a city. The other was a metaphorical meaning referring to leadership and authority. This is what we mean today by head and headship. But once again, these last two uses of head were not the normal ways the word was used in New Testament times.

Traditionally, we have interpreted the word "head" both here and elsewhere in the New Testament as leadership and authority. This, of course, leads to a male predominance interpretation, which then is read back to the creation accounts. An interpretation that is confirmed by the hierarchy mentioned in this passage. God has authority over Jesus, Jesus has authority over man, and man has authority over woman.

But what if we use the two more familiar meanings as we read this passage. Then head refers to one's literal head and also to the source or the origin of one's being. If that were the case then the passage is not to be interpreted from an hierarchical point of reference, but from an historical point of reference. Jesus is the source of man because Jesus created man first (that is, chronologically before Eve, not predominantly or authoritatively before Eve) and man is the source of woman because she was formed from man's rib, and finally, God is the source of Jesus in terms of His incarnation. This interpretation has much going for it because it follows the order of Paul's sequence better. A hierarchical interpretation must contend with the fact that Paul's sequence seems strange. It would be more natural to speak of God being the head of Jesus, Jesus being the head of man, and man being the head of woman. And this interpretation does justice to the natural reading of Genesis 2:20b–25 as discussed earlier.

Note the shift from creation and protocol to salvation in Jesus Christ in verse 11. From the perspective of being in the Lord, men and women are equal. They are mutually dependent on each other (Is this why we must mutually submit to each other in Christ [see Ephesians 5:21]?) and totally dependent on God.

Paul's use of the word "proper" in verse 13 seems to fall short of a universal command. In fact, Paul makes *us* the judge of such things!

Once again, whatever Paul is saying in reaction to whatever was happening in Corinth at this time, we can say that our freedom in Christ does not abolish the distinctions between the sexes nor does it call for wanton disregard of the way that a culture expresses those distinctions. But then again, neither does it prohibit women from praying and prophesying in church.

1 Corinthians 14:26–40

This is one of the classic passages used to irrefutably restrict women from certain ministries. Is that indeed what the passage is saying? My personal approach to Scripture is that it is infallible. My humble approach to human interpretation, including my own, is that it is not.

In 1 Corinthians 11:5 Paul specifically states that women pray and prophesy. Does he then contradict himself three chapters later? How could she both pray and prophesy and remain silent at the same time?

Theories abound!

1. Paul is hopelessly confused and cannot be taken seriously.
2. The praying and prophesying that Paul's speaking of in chapter 11 isn't in the context of a congregational setting. When the whole congregation gets together women must be silent. This is a universal principle as seen in the fact that Paul appeals to the witness of the practice of all the congregations, the Law, and what is considered decent. But many students of the Bible feel that Paul is clearly referring to congregational worship in chapter 11.
3. The words *"for it is disgraceful for a woman to speak in the church"* are more a statement of social fact than biblical principle. Paul was emphatic that nothing would become a stumbling block to the cause of Christ. After just stating that women could pray and prophesy, with the socially appropriate attire, he goes on to say in some cases they shouldn't even speak at all for the sake of the Gospel. Therefore, Paul's words are considered

situational and not universal. In other words, in cultures where there are no social taboos against women involved in public settings, then a women's involvement would not be restricted, but encouraged.

4. The women in the Corinthian church, specifically, were an unruly bunch. In fact, much of the church's confusion was caused by them. Coming from pagan mystery religions, where women may have exercised a vocal and brash hold on leadership, it seems that they were taking this model right into the church. Obviously, Paul didn't want that happening. So Paul gives some pretty strong words to curb this problem. So, Paul is not against women praying and prophesying in the church. What he is against is prayers and prophecies that resemble the pagan culture around the church. So, Paul's instructions are considered situational and not universal.

5. In verse 33b–35 Paul is quoting the antagonists in Corinth. Therefore, if Greek had "quotation marks," Paul would have used them here. In effect, verse 36 would start with an astonished "What!?" or "Nonsense!" or "Come on!" or "Who are you kidding?!" This is gathered from the little Greek disjunction "e." Paul used this disjunction—indicating a strong reaction, even rejection, to what proceeds it—several times in 1 Corinthians. For example, see 6:8–9, 6:15b–16, 9:9–10.

Proponents of this approach point to the "fact" that women did participate in the life and ministry of the church. For example, in Acts 18:26 Priscilla, along with her husband (her name uncustomarily is mentioned first), taught and corrected Apollos. In Romans 16:1–2 Phoebe was a deaconess (or simple female deacon). Junias, who in Romans 16:7 is referred to by Paul as *"outstanding among the apostles."* Or Mary, Tryphena and Tryphosa, *"who work hard in the Lord"* (Romans 16:6,12). And Euodia and Syntyche *"contended at [Paul's] side in the case of the gospel"* (Philippians 4:2–3). The advocates of this view also question why Paul would appeal to the Law as a witness when he said we were free from the Law (especially the ceremonial and cultic aspects of the Law). And who says that it is disgraceful for a woman to speak in church? Are these the words of Paul or the Judaizers, for example, whom Paul was constantly battling?

John Calvin put it this way:

> The discerning reader should come to the decision that the things that Paul is dealing with here are indifferent, neither good nor bad; and that they are forbidden only because they work against seemliness and edification.[19]

1 TIMOTHY 2:11–15

Once again, we find ourselves in one of the much-debated passages. Is Paul saying that women are not allowed to teach or have authority over a man ever? Many say yes. Historically, the church has agreed, especially considering Paul's reference to the creational order.

Others point out that there is only one main verb in the passage— *"a woman should learn."* All other verbs and adverbs are subordinate to it. So, what if a woman learns in quietness and full submission? Would she then be permitted after learning to teach and have authority over men? They suggest she would.

They deal with the reference to the Fall not as an order of creation, but as an order of education. Yes, Adam was formed first and then Eve. But does this make him superior? Our original look at the creation account would suggest not necessarily so.

Maybe the reference to being formed first is a reference to the fact that Adam received the command directly from the Lord and Eve received it secondhand through Adam. This would not make her morally inferior, just educationally handicapped. Which is the main point of this passage in 1 Timothy in the first place. Look at what happened when Eve had a faulty education. The whole world was led into sin. Too bad she hadn't learned her lesson better. Or too bad Adam hadn't taught the lesson better. So just like Eve, unqualified people can get the church

---

[19] Dr. Ralph F. Wilson, *Jesus Walk*, "13. Prophecy and Ministry by the Holy Spirit (1 Corinthians 14)." Accessed: September 19, 2014 (http://www.jesuswalk.com/1corinthians/13_prophecy.htm#_ftn547). Quoting John Calvin, *Commentary on Corinthians*, translation from C.K. Barrett, *1 Corinthians*, p. 333.

into a lot of trouble. But what happens if they become qualified? What happens if they learn their lessons?

Can they then teach?

1 TIMOTHY 3:1–13

Here we go again? Many say this passage obviously, explicitly, unambiguously says a woman cannot function in the role of elder. Deacon maybe; elder definitely not. Once again, the weight of history stands behind them. Or so it may seem...

Yet, what is the history that really counts here? Is it the history of the church in general or the history of the Ephesian church in particular? Historically, what was happening in the Ephesian church? Paul had prophesied that the church would be attacked both externally from wolves and internally from heretics (Acts 20:17–38). From 1 Timothy we get the sense that this prophecy came true. The spiritual storm had hit the Ephesian church with gale force. And Paul leaves Timothy in Ephesus as his apostolic representative (1 Timothy 1:3–7) to deal with the crisis. Timothy, it seems, along with Titus in Crete (Titus 1:5), were not the permanent pastors of these churches. They were ambassadors of Paul commissioned to deal with the problems that arose in these churches. Their very presence suggests that something very bad was happening in the churches and that it took extra strong measures to deal with it. In effect, Paul is imposing "martial law" in the churches to restore order for the sake of survival.

Other questions to consider when working through 1 Timothy and Titus: the question of whatever happened to Paul's emphasis on spiritual gifts as a means of determining ministry fitfulness? Or what about the servant-supportive nature of leadership in the church? The tone of these letters seems to point to a leadership team that is one of top-down control, rather than one of bottom-up support. Or what if you're a man and not married? What if you're a married man and have no kids? What if you're a married man and your kids are unruly? Can these men serve as elders? That certainly reduces the amount of eligible people for the ministry of elder. Yet, if we are to remain logically consistent, we may need to come to such conclusions. Otherwise, we may be guilty of holding a double standard.

The question then is, is this to be the normative model for the church of all times? Since Paul was soon to die and he had to pass the baton to the next generations of leaders (like Timothy and Titus), was this his way of changing the leadership style to fit the impending post-apostolic situation? Or is this a remedial, corrective solution for a church that was near the brink of extinction? Were the highly stringent and limiting conditions for leadership demanded in order to deal with a situation where only the most qualified—that is, those who had a proven track record at home—could possibly serve? And finally, what if a church doesn't find itself in such dire straits as the church in Ephesus; are Paul's words intended for this church?

GALATIANS 3:28

This passage deals with the three great divisions of the ancient world: the division between Jews and Greeks, slaves and free, men and women. For example, some Jewish males greeted each day praying, "Lord, I thank you that I am not a Gentile, a slave, or a woman." Paul, however, says that faith in Jesus overcomes all of these divisions and makes all believers one in Christ. Could this passage give us Paul's ideal, and therefore ultimate goal for life in God's new Kingdom?

Actually, Paul's treatment on slavery is helpful to consider in this discussion. This comes from Peter Fitch's paper prepared for The Association of Vineyard Churches in Canada:

> The way that Paul teaches about the issue of slavery probably provides a framework for us to understand his limitations on women in the problem passages. If he had challenged the situation of slavery directly, Christianity would have been seen by everyone in the first century as another movement to free the slaves of the Roman Empire. Each one of these was squashed by Rome's imperial might, yet what Paul did proved to be more effective in the long run. He destroyed slavery, not by forbidding it, but by teaching slaves and masters to love each other as brothers in the Lord. In the Western world, the fight to free slaves was led by people like Britain's William Wilberforce

in the 19th century precisely because he understood what Paul was teaching and was committed to it. Similarly, we believe that Paul dealt realistically with the difficulties of his culture's view of women in the problem passages, but that he sowed seeds of a better way in Galatians 3:28.[20]

SUMMARY

There's a line in "Joy to the World" that I love: "He comes to make His blessings flow far as the curse is found." If male domination is part of the curse and not necessarily part of God's good creation, then shouldn't our re-creation in Christ begin the process of reversing this area of the curse? Shouldn't we allow both men and women to express their full freedom in Christ using whatever gifts He sovereignly dispenses for His glory and for the upbuilding of the church?

Can John Wesley and the Pentecostal churches and the Salvation Army serve as a model to follow? Not a model of the slippery slope that leads to all kinds of heresy, but a model of a straight road that leads to greater unity and ministry.

There is neither Jew not Greek, slave nor free, male nor female, for you are all one in Christ Jesus. (Galatians 3:28)

* * *

Upon returning home from Karl House's office, I quickly read this report. The fact that God led me to his office when the only written material there was the paper about women in ministry seemed significant. Did this report reflect God's heart? Once again, I wondered: *Why me? Why now? Why the change of heart on God's part?*

---

[20] Peter Fitch, *Women in Ministry*, Official Position Paper of the Association of Vineyard Churches, Canada, submitted and accepted 2000.

Music can change the world because it can change people.

—Bono, musician and humanitarian

eight

UNDERSTANDING OUR TIMES

Years ago, God admonished me for wasting time researching the subject of women and the church. Are present-day churches expending needless time and energy debating the matter? I personally know several elders boards that have invested countless hours over the past couple of decades hashing and rehashing this secondary issue. And hashing again. No doubt, there are more important matters for the bride of Christ, the church, to be addressing at this particular juncture: the disintegration of the family unit, the pain caused by addiction and abuse, the problem of pornography, the prevalence of human trafficking, the dangers facing the youth of today (including the destructive drug culture, and with it the proliferation of violence and crime), not to mention, of course, the over-secularization of the church. At the opposite end of the spectrum: the expansion of the Kingdom of God, the need for personal holiness (including a greater emphasis on the importance and power of prayer), a deeper commitment to social justice (particularly the needs of the homeless, poor, and marginalized), the call to servanthood (as opposed to the celebration of celebrity), and always, a greater understanding of the Spirit-filled life. In a nutshell, the advance of Kingdom good.

In our current generation, is Kingdom good hampered by the church's position regarding women in ministry? Much of the church hangs on to traditional roles for daughters of the King, while in the broader culture, women are free to run a corporation or country, spearhead a writers' conference, even captain the *Starship Voyager*, one of the fastest, most powerful starships in all of Starfleet. Built in 2371, the *Voyager* is, of course, fictional, but this television series is made for today's audience and is indicative of where women are headed. Remember the Jetsons, the futuristic family of Hanna-Barbera fame? Well, all those unbelievable technological means of communication are in vogue today. Change is unavoidable.

As I write this paragraph, my attention is captured by a radio announcement about a rule change regarding ascension to the throne of England: no matter the gender, the firstborn can now wear the crown—the Maple Crown, as far as we Canadians are concerned. What's more, heirs to the throne are free to marry Roman Catholics for the first time in over six hundred years. "This is a modernization that makes perfect sense," announced James Moore, Minister of Canadian Heritage and Official Languages.

There's a whole lotta fence-movin' goin' on! Society is moving with rapidity toward lessening inequalities and loosening chains of prejudice and oppression. Is God displeased that His people refuse to move the gender fence, or at best, still straddle the pickets? That's not a comfortable place for anyone. A line from "O Holy Night," one of my favourite Christmas carols, speaks of God's ideal for His redeemed: "In His name all oppression shall cease."

The prophet Isaiah speaks to this issue as well.

Is not this the kind of fasting I have chosen: to loose the chains of injustice and untie the cords of the yoke, to set the oppressed free and break every yoke? Is it not to share your food with the hungry and to provide the poor wanderer with shelter—when you see the naked, to clothe him, and not to turn away from your own flesh and blood? Then your light will break forth like the dawn, and your healing will quickly appear; then your righteousness will go before you, and the glory of the Lord will be your rear guard."' Then you will call, and the Lord will answer; you will cry for help, and he will say: Here am I.

If you do away with the yoke of oppression, with the pointing finger and malicious talk, and if you spend yourselves in behalf of the hungry and satisfy the needs of the oppressed, then your light will rise in the darkness, and your night will become like the noonday. The Lord will guide you always; he will satisfy your needs in a sun-scorched land and will strengthen your frame. You will be like a well-watered garden, like a spring whose waters never fail. (Isaiah 58:6–11)

The Bible itself promotes cultural competence, addressing the need to respond to specific cultural settings. Consider the mighty men of King David: *"men of Issachar, who understood the times and knew what Israel should do—200 chiefs, with all their relatives under their command"* (1 Chronicles 12:32). David himself is said to have *"served God's purpose in his own generation"* (Acts 13:36a). Perhaps God feels we are not serving our generation adequately when women are left sitting on the sidelines (ridin' the pine, as we say in softball circles), gifts underdeveloped, potential untapped.

Religious organizations in particular are resistant to change. Tampering with beloved tradition is considered sin by some, sometimes causing tradition to become a stifling substitute for religion itself, deafening our ears to the voice of the living God, hardening our hearts to the work of His Spirit.

When I moved from the Alliance church clear across Peterborough to Auburn Bible Chapel, I had a hard time accepting a new format for the communion service, for the Breaking of Bread. I appreciated that the Lord's Supper was acknowledged on a weekly basis—it *is* the sign of the New Covenant (Luke 22:20)—however, in my opinion, because it happened so often it didn't seem to be conducted with the same care, passion, and awe I was accustomed to. Years ago, when my father, an elder at the Cobourg Christian and Missionary Alliance Church, prayed for the wine representing the blood of Jesus, it was an event in itself.

My selfish attitude hampered my worship experience more than I'd like to admit. And furthermore, what difference did it make if everyone partook of the bread and juice immediately, as opposed to tarrying one for another, the way I'd been taught in my denomination's monthly remembrances, the way Paul instructed the church at Corinth (1 Corinthians 11:23–34). I should have been focusing on Jesus and His great sacrifice—that of giving up His life on my behalf—instead of on my silly sacrifice—that of giving up my precious traditions. I had no idea how tightly wound, how tightly bound to tradition I'd become (tighter than an airport sandwich) until this eye-opening experience. I'd forgotten that the true heart of worship isn't what we receive for ourselves, but what we offer up to God, who should be the focus of our worship. Once I made this "audience of one" attitudinal adjustment, I had much less of a problem.

Yet once more, this New Testament passage raises a question: was Paul addressing a self-discipline problem in the Corinthian church or were his instructions regarding the distribution of the elements at the Lord's Supper intended as a pattern to be followed by Jesus' followers until we all gather at the Marriage Supper of the Lamb?

When you really think about it, the Bible is very big on change. Abraham was asked to leave everything behind and go (Genesis 12:1). Rahab, a harlot of Jericho, aided the Israelite spies, drastically changing her allegiance and subsequently her life (Joshua 2:1–6; Matthew 1:5; Hebrews 11:31). Mild-mannered fishermen were asked to abandon mending their mesh in order to hang out with the Messiah. He, in turn, empowered them to become bold, courageous fishers of men (Luke 5:6–11). Mary of Bethany, sister of Martha, was welcomed by Jesus into the men's part of the household and included in the teaching and training session that took place at His feet (Luke 10:38–42), a radical change from centuries of Jewish tradition. For

> rather should the words of Torah be burned than entrusted to a woman… whoever teaches his daughter the Torah is like one who teaches her obscenity.[21]

Such a list must also include Saul of Tarsus, whose conversion not only changed his name to Paul, but also the course of his life and that of

---

[21] Rabbi Eliezer, *Mishnah,* Satah 3:4.

all Christendom (Acts 9:1–28). The Gospel of Luke, however, records the greatest, most wonderful, most powerful transformation in all of history.

Why do you look for the living among the dead? He is not here; he has risen! (Luke 24:5b–6a)

This information was directed to the women who came to the tomb, the women who were the first to see and communicate with the risen Saviour.

It's highly significant that Jesus first appeared to women, enlisting Mary Magdalene to *"Go... and tell"* (John 20:17). If I wanted to fabricate the fact that Jesus rose from the dead and concoct a fictional eye witness account, I would never have selected a small group of women to be the initial witness. At the time, a woman's word was considered invalid in a court of law. This countercultural detail is not only indicative of how highly Christ valued women, it also lends further credence to the resurrection story.

In Funk & Wagnalls, one definition of an apostle is "the earliest or foremost advocate of a cause."[22] That makes these women "apostles to the apostles."

It was Mary Magdalene, Joanna, Mary the mother of James, and the others with them who told this to the apostles. But they did not believe the women, because their words seemed to them like nonsense. (Luke 24:10–11)

Despite what you may think of my words today, I'm not advocating that Christians accept change *carte blanche.* We're not to embrace sinful actions that will lead to the degradation of society; we're called to be salt and light (Matthew 5:13–14) in order to preserve and illuminate that which is holy and just and right. Although we live in this fallen world, we're called to live according to Kingdom values and not embrace every

---

[22] *Funk & Wagnalls Standard Desk Dictionary, Volume One* (New York, NY: Harper & Row Publishers, Inc., 1984). 29.

erroneous way. A little *mutatis mutandis*—change only in the things that need changing—is in order here. As well as a great deal of wisdom!

Did God want me to gain more wisdom and accumulate a broader body of experience before I tackled such an important project as women and the church? Or perhaps mature in my faith and gain experience in partnering with the Holy Spirit so this book would be Spirit-driven as opposed to "Judi's judgement on the matter," no doubt a paltry point of view? At the writers' conference, Stiller spoke on the necessity of partnering with the Spirit:

> The Holy Spirit is not only the agent that gives wisdom, inspiration and insight, but He also takes what we say and applies it to the heart of the reader. As writers we are dependent on the Spirit from start to finish.[23]

I know that my work, my life, is dependent on the work and life of the Holy Spirit, and I have confidence that the Holy Spirit can work through me, giving me inspiration in order to accomplish God's purposes. At the same time, an element of fear lingered. I considered the elders of the church my friends. They firmly believed they were honouring God's Word in their strong opinions regarding women's subordinate place in the church. If I was to write a book about this issue, how would it be received? How would *I* be received? Again, would people think I was promoting my own agenda, when all I really wanted to do was be an obedient servant of the Sovereign Lord?

Although I feared rocking the Brethren boat a little (or rather, trying to move the Brethren fence), I feared disobeying God—a lot. I came up with an idea that would hopefully keep my Heavenly Father happy and get me off the obedience hook. If I couldn't actually move the fence, perhaps I could at least make it a little rickety for the benefit of the next generation. I decided to keep myself out of the picture; I would write a letter to the elders on behalf of a young female friend.

I don't remember all the details, but I asked the church to give more speaking time to a YWAM (Youth with a Mission) missionary who was

---

[23] Dr. Brian Stiller, *Write! Canada, Plenary 2*, 2009, compact disc.

stationed at a snowboarders' Discipleship Training School in Davos, in the heart of the Swiss Alps—something more than the five minutes usually allotted her when she came home for the summer months. Passionate and Spirit-empowered, this young woman captivated when she spoke, evidenced by the quieting of the congregation, the smiles, the leaning forward. She was required to solicit her own financial support and I believed she was deeply hampered by being female. She certainly didn't have the same platform to speak as young men in similar scenarios. And ministry leaders often lament the fact that they are overburdened, overworked. Why not make the load lighter on our own leadership by letting her have the entire thirty or forty minutes of preaching time some Sunday morning? We could even call it "sharing," if that would make it more palatable.

There, I've obeyed God, I told myself, finally mustering up the nerve to press the send button on my computer, forwarding the email to lead pastor Jay Lehman and asking him to pass it on to the rest of the elders board. I'd written about the church's oppression of women (not my words, but God's).

Meanwhile, I was speaking here and there, working as a literacy volunteer, leading Bible studies, writing for a Christian periodical, and praying with "my ladies" on a regular basis.[24] Surely, I was doing enough for God. He really didn't expect me to do much more regarding women and the church. I mean, I'd done what I could. What could I, one semi-retired, middle-aged woman, expect to accomplish anyway?

---

[24] Praying with this Spirit-inspired group of intrepid warriors on Tuesday mornings had become top priority for me.

In a fiddler's house, all are dancers.

—Rwandan proverb

nine

CHANGE THE WORLD WITH WORDS?

In the spring of 2011, a few months before The Word Guild's annual writers' conference, I felt God nudging me to register. Once again, Write! Canada would be held on the beautiful grounds of the Guelph Bible Conference Centre. But I really didn't have a lot of extra money and my husband was retiring soon. His official retirement date was the first day of the conference. How would that be fair? Taking off the very day he retired? Shouldn't the two of us have had a celebratory dinner or something? Yet deep down, I knew God wanted me to go. Initially, I thought it was because of my involvement with *A Second Cup of Hot Apple Cider*,[25] the best-selling, award-winning anthology, but that turned out to be only a small part.

"You'll have to change my husband's retirement date and find me free accommodation," I told God. "And... I'd like a room to myself so there's no snoring." I tilted my head heavenward and laughed. "You know what a horrible sleeper I am."

After work, a few days later, my husband burst through the side door into the kitchen. "They want me to change my retirement date. They want me to stay on a couple more weeks, just until negotiations are over. What do you think?"

---

[25] N.J. Lindquist and Wendy Elaine Nelles, eds., *A Second Cup of Hot Apple Cider* (Markham, ON: That's Life! Communications, 2011).

"That's fine with me," I stated, matter-of-factly. My shoulders shrugged indifferently. "Whatever ya' think works best."

Inwardly, I was dancing.

Free accommodation took a little longer to materialize, but sure enough, by the time the conference arrived I'd scored a room in a University of Guelph townhouse for the weekend. Not merely a room of my own, but an entire floor. (I'm not anti-social, by the way, just a very light sleeper.) I know staying onsite is preferable, for schmoozing and such and taking part in late-night readings and early-morning prayer, but this particular year, this worked for me.

Contributors to *A Second Cup of Hot Apple Cider,* all of us members of The Word Guild, assembled for a photo shoot on Thursday afternoon. Thursday evening, Tim Huff, winner of the Grace Irwin Award, Canada's largest literary prize for writers who are Christian, addressed an eager group of writers and editors gathered from all across Canada. His signature ball cap was in place, pulled snug over long, blondish-brown hair, and his whiskery neck mantle was pronounced, allowing him to smoothly blend with those he ministers to. I talked to Tim later that evening, telling him how much I had enjoyed *Bent Hope,* his collection of gripping narratives relating to his work with the homeless and struggling street youth of Toronto.

"I read it from time to time," I elaborated. "It reminds me of God's grace, and mercy and love, and helps keep me compassionate when I do literacy work with some of the tougher kids."

While we spoke, a tear formed in the corner of one of Tim's eyes and I sensed how deeply committed this man was to helping those who've been damaged by the circumstances of life.

At one point in Tim's message, he informed us about his latest project, The Hope Exchange. Its message: bring hope, serve well, and celebrate all endeavours.[26]

Personally, I don't know anyone whose journey of service more beautifully calls to mind the Isaiah 58:6–11 passage in the previous chapter. Huff seems to understand God's heart. Plus, his writing is

---

[26] The Hope Exchange merged with The National Roundtable on Poverty and Homelessness in 2012 to form T.H.E. StreetLevel Network.

really great. His words, carefully strung—like pearls. And that's another thing I like to do from time to time: immerse myself in the work of great authors. Not to copy their style, but to get a feel for… well, what constitutes great writing.

I bought Tim's latest book, *Dancing with Dynamite*, and asked him to autograph the cover page: "Judi—All the best in all life's adventures! God bless!"

Little did we know that I was about to embark on one of those adventures that very night.

Upon arriving at the townhouse complex, just minutes from the conference grounds, I was thrilled to discover that my bedroom was bedecked with colourful birthday banners, cards, streamers, and balloons. Apparently, Sherri Tedford, the young woman who had generously loaned me her room for the weekend, had recently celebrated her birthday. Her three housemates had decorated it and she hadn't yet had a chance to remove the birthday banter. Our immeasurably great God not only found me free accommodation in Guelph, but a room that would acknowledge and celebrate my birthday. Born on Father's Day in 1956, with the Cobourg Salvation Army Band playing "My Faith Looks Up to Thee" outside my mother's hospital window, I would turn fifty-five in the morning, knowing my Heavenly Father was looking down on me in Guelph, growing my faith and enfolding me in His love. *Yes, God is beyond amazing,* I decided as I snuggled under the covers with Huff's new book, my birthday present to myself.

"This is a beautiful book about meetings," Jean Vanier begins in the foreword. His second paragraph continues, "This is a book of hope and healing."[27]

Vanier would know about such things. He's the founder of the International Federation of L'Arche Communities, the

> network of homes where people with developmental disabilities, volunteers and staff live together in community. Those we lock

---

[27] Tim Huff, *Dancing with Dynamite: Celebrating Against the Odds* (Pickering, ON: Castle Quay Books, 2010), 11.

away and think worthless, he says, have the power to teach and even to heal us.[28]

Huff himself pens the prologue, speaking about outsiders. And belonging.

In minutes, I experienced all of this—a supernatural meeting with my Abba Father, who desires to bring hope, healing, and belonging to all His children. Especially young men like Oscar, and women in the church, like me.

What follows is the first story in Huff's book:

* * *

DANCE WHILE YOU CAN

"Doctor John Langdon Down, 1866. Do you know him? Do you? Ah, c'mon, do you or don't you?" Oscar interrogated me the moment I walked through the front door for the first time, before I could even begin to squeeze out any kind of a greeting.

"Oscar, at least let him get through the door and meet you," the on-site nurse reprimanded him as she nodded and smiled at me.

But Oscar was relentless.

"He invented idiots and imbeciles, that Doctor John Langdon Down did. Idiots and imbeciles, woo-hoo!" he cackled, and ran away down the hall, giggling.

"No, he didn't! He classified them a long, long time ago! It meant something different way back then! We've had this discussion countless times, Oscar! Those are not nice words anymore!" the sweet nurse shouted out from the kitchen with a reluctant grin.

Then she turned to me and cocked her head. "Welcome. You must be Tim. That is…" She sighed and cleared her throat, "Um, Oscar."

In the distance, Oscar's muffled voice continued from behind his bedroom door. "Idiots and imbeciles, idiots and imbeciles, woo-hoo! That Doctor John Langdon Down was something else!"

---

[28] Ibid., 11–12.

Oscar was pear shaped and barely four feet tall at age 22. In all my years of working in group homes and what were then called "special needs facilities and camps," I never met another individual so aware, knowledgeable and hilarious about his own complex challenges and genetic makeup. He knew more about Down syndrome than any of the staff. I was in college at the time, studying syndromes, genetics and cognitive development as part of completing a developmental service worker diploma. I had many part-time jobs, placements and volunteer positions in residential and institutional settings throughout my college years. However, none of these experiences, or any formal schooling, tutored me the way Oscar unintentionally did while I was serving at his group home.

Nothing was out of bounds for Oscar. Especially around the topic of Down syndrome, which he studied endlessly and had his own take on. Mealtimes were served up with Oscar's generous series of single and out-of-context words and sentences, spoken with a full mouth, between bites.

"Action T-4. The Nazis would have murdered me."

Spoonful of corn.

"Genetic material on the 21st chromosome, that's the issue."

Forkful of beans.

"Nondisjunction. Nondisjunction."

Swig of milk.

But for me, Oscar was at his fascinating best when he used his knowledge for sly comedic effect.

He loved to put the flat back of his head against the wall and say, "Look at me, coming from out of nowhere." Or he'd playfully push me as though provoking fisticuffs and say, "You think I'm mentally retarded, don't you! Don't you! Well, put your dukes up! I'll show you who's retarded!" And one of his favourite things to do was to stick out his long, thick, pointed tongue as far as he could and say, "You don't even want to know the damage this can do."

I never sensed he really meant it in any sexual way—he was just very aware of the difference in his tongue from everyone else's. And he was proud of it. Still, it always got him a half-hearted scolding from staff and a very terse "You're gross" from the other residents. Particularly from Sheila, who not so secretly had a crush on him. As he did her.

But at his best, naughtiest, and everything in-between, one thing was clear: Oscar owned this home. His mood set the tone for everyone for the entire day. On days when he was grumpy, he possessed the power to bring grey clouds right into the room with him. He could design the day with a woeful grunt, or pattern the next 24 hours off a dramatic shrug and snort. And if you didn't share his disdain, he kept coming at you until you did.

But this was rare. At his usual best, he was a beacon. His quotes were "the" repeated and keeper ones. His laugh was infectious, his voice was dynamic, and his presence was electric. When he was on and in the room, everyone felt more alive.

At no time was this more evident than when any kind of celebration was at hand. Oscar was Brother Birthday, Captain Christmas and the tooth fairy's sidekick all rolled into one. No event was too small to turn into a party. During my time there, Oscar organized and resided over house parties for everything from a funeral and wake for a baby robin that fell from a backyard tree, to a graduation ceremony for one of the residents who learned to tie her shoes. And not just spur-of-the-moment parties. That was unthinkable. He wanted to create working committees, delegate responsibilities and make "coming event" posters. He was an all-or-nothing guy, who always chose "all."

It was during a dry celebration season on the calendar that Oscar hatched a new party scheme. Between April and May, there were no real holiday events or house birthdays to commemorate, so Oscar lobbied for a dance party. He pitched a Sadie Hawkins dance, a costume ball and a luau, all to no avail. Each one considered somewhat lofty for a household of seven. But he met the staff halfway with a more modest festivity in the form of an agreed-upon spring dance.

Anything to break out the "blue boogie dogs." That was what Oscar called his special blue high-top sneakers, which he saved solely for dance occasions.

A date was chosen and circled on the large kitchen calendar, and the one-week count-down began. And so did Oscar's very serious and thorough to-do lists. He organized a decorating committee, a music committee, a refreshments committee, an advertising committee, a greeters' committee, and on and on. There was even a wardrobe committee responsible for making sure that everyone came in spring attire. While most of the staff and residents had to sit on three or four committees, simply because there were as many committees as people, Oscar sat on and chaired them all, as the self-imposed and proclaimed event coordinator and master of ceremonies.

The end of day six came slowly. Oscar had been a taskmaster from beginning to end, and throughout the week there was never any allowance for conversation about anything that was not in one way or another related to the spring dance. As bedtime for the residents finally rolled around on that final day, I was putting away towels in the hallway linen closet, right across from Oscar's room. Those moments became some of the most profound in my lifetime. It was there that I could hear Oscar saying his bedtime prayers.

Oscar prayed for God to help him sleep, because he was so excited. Then he went on to explain to God that he was not as excited as on Christmas Eve, but more excited than the night before St. Patrick's day—kind of somewhere in between. He lost focus and began talking about how excited he gets on Christmas Eve, knowing Santa and his eight reindeer are on the way (adding, "nine if you count Rudolph, but he is not one of the originals, so you can't always count on it"), then caught himself and assured God that he was just as excited that it was the baby Jesus' birthday too.

He got his prayers on track with an "Okay, Heavenly Father, back to the dance…," and prayed for each committee one by one. He prayed that the Kool-Aid would not be too sweet, and still not too watered down. And that there would be enough of the red and orange Kool-Aid, because no one liked the green stuff. He prayed that people would really think through what to wear and not just show up in "any old thing."

My silent position was all but compromised with muffled laughter when he prayed that God would help him remember all his best dance moves, and that Sheila would like them.

But the best was saved for last. He closed by praying for each resident, one by one. Then each person on staff, one by one. Name by name. That each one of us would "have a fun time and forget our worries for a little while." And in that very moment, I could feel Oscar's heart beating in rhythm with God's own in a way I was sure mine never had. That Oscar could pray such a thing for me, while knowing only too well—and better than most—all of the obstacles and challenges in his life, completely overwhelmed me.

He said his amen, and then in a manner I could only imagine made the maker of the sun, moon and stars Himself chuckle, he added, "P.S. Heavenly Father, I think I offended Sheila today. If I did, I am sorry. If not, then never mind."

Brilliant.

Finally, the big day came. A bright, sunny Sunday. As beautiful as it was, the morning was nothing but agonizing for Oscar—which translated into agony for everyone—as the 2 p.m. start time took forever to arrive. But when it did, Oscar did not miss a beat, and did not disappoint. He left his clipboard behind and put on his finest party hat. He worked the room like an ambassador. Glad-handing and small-talking like an aristocrat who'd invited everyone who's anyone. He was jolly with big shy Paulie. He was buddy-buddy with sporty Clifford. He was gentle with mousey Alita. And he was charming and smooth with Sheila, of course.

And he danced! Oh, he danced! Not simply like people do when attending a dance party. Oscar danced the way songwriters describe dancing in heaven when they talk about being in the presence of God. His tiny eyes were shut tight, his little hands would wiggle in the air, and his head would bob to one side while his hips bounced to the other. He was extraordinary. And at the start of every song and several times throughout, he would open his eyes and take note of anyone not moving to the beat and shout at them, "Dance while you can! Dance while you can!"

Because we knew he would dance nonstop and put his complex body at risk, we had convinced him that there should be a "socializing break" between songs. He loved the idea, and thought it was so he could schmooze and make sure everyone was having a good time. And that he did. But when that music started up, he went into full groove.

With the sly advantage of chairing the music committee, Oscar had sorted out a different dance move for every song, calling them out by name as he performed them. The blue boogie dogs were more than alive and well. Somewhere between the hustle and the mashed potato, he had even calculated a moment to invite Sheila to slow dance with him. He was in his glory.

Three twenty-five p.m. came, and it was nearly time for the party to end. Oscar crawled onto the coffee table, a big wet mess. His hair was standing on end, one side of his shirt was untucked, and he had cookie crumbs and Kool-Aid stains on his face. But once he balanced himself on the small oak table, he was nothing shy of the emperor.

"I'd like to thank everyone for attending the first annual spring dance," he said with great distinction.

I looked at another staff member and smiled. No one had agreed on the "annual" part. He continued by thanking each committee, and then launched into his final announcement.

"As a special treat," he continued, "we will end with my presentation of the electric slide."

He pointed at Sheila, who he had prearranged would push play on the tape deck, on cue.

And it happened, just as planned. Click. And he bounced off the coffee table, boogying to the theme from *Saturday Night Fever*. And electric slide he did. Along with every other dance move he had seen, heard of, or could make up in the moment, all the while calling out to every wallflower and person not bobbing to the beat, "Dance while you can! Dance while you can!"

The party ended, noted by all in attendance as the best house party ever. And truly it was that, and more. Of all the parties I have ever attended in my lifetime, none has ever been more memorable or more vivid in my mind.

Oscar ate well that night. He laughed and played "remember when" all evening about the party as though it had happened years ago. He had a bath, had his snack and said his prayers, like every other night. Woke up to porridge, half a banana and orange juice in his favourite Batman cup, and prepared for his day program like every other weekday morning. He took his lunch out of the fridge, said his goodbyes and stood on the front stoop to wait for his bus. The little bus pulled up at 8:45 a.m. and Oscar was on his way. Just as he had done countless times before.

But Oscar never came back. He had a seizure while at his day program. This was not uncommon. But through a series of complexities, this particularly severe seizure had great ramifications to his congenital heart defects. It was later diagnosed that it was in no way linked to overexertion of any kind. These complications and threats had been looming his entire life. In fact, most of the scares around his past chest and heart pains came the very few times he was too *inactive*.

I only worked at that particular group home for another month or so. The first week after Oscar was gone, the grief was palpable. No one knew what to do or what to say. Or so I thought. We on staff tried to speak comfort and reassurance to the residents, but nothing we said hit the mark. For me, the world didn't look the same, and God seemed a thief. My attempts were authentic, but my heart was in betrayal. That was until big, bumbling Paulie stopped me midway through one of my lost causes, babbling sentences about it being okay to cry. He put his heavy arm around me and simply said, "We all hurt the same."

I had taken no cues from the renowned L'Arche communities around the world. I was dug deep in the "us and them" of staff and resident—titles created by humans that often surrender the most significant notions of humanity and godliness. Ones that can thwart the opportunity for authentic community when given too much power.

Paulie walked away. But not before I noticed a small, nuanced behaviour. He stepped very gently through the hallway, past the side door. I wondered why. It was very uncharacteristic. I watched him closely but could not put it all together until I looked past the furniture obstructing my view.

There it was. The answer. Not just how they were coping, but how they were healing.

Oscar's special blue high-top running shoes were left at the side door. They had not moved since the dance. And they weren't going to.

Without anyone speaking a word, Oscar's dearest friends had very purposefully left his special shoes untouched as a memorial to him. There was little or no access to gravesites and tombstone visits in their world. As staff, thick in policies and academic responses, our attempts to truly provide comfort were feeble at best. But they knew better anyway. There was more life and healing found in looking upon those worn sneakers, and pondering their purpose and owner, than any stone monument could have ever offered.

I will never forget the last day I worked at the home. I came from the basement without being noticed, only to find Sheila sitting cross-legged only inches in front of the shoes, weeping. Then laughing. Weeping. Then laughing. Experiencing grief as she should. And life as she must.

Oscar didn't just know what the key to life was. He didn't simply sense what God really wants from us. He lived and laughed and loved all in the centre of it, being this:

Not only should we all dance while we can. Of course. For Oscar that would've been completely obvious. But that we find ways for others to do the same. Oscar was thrilled to dance and was on fire that everyone would have the same chance.

But his greatest joy always came when everyone did.

Ironically, the influential and controversial nineteenth-century German philosopher Friedrich Wilhelm Nietzsche, who turned his back on his faith at a young age while studying theology, and who eventually ended up incapacitated by complete insanity, said it best: "I would believe only in a God that knows how to dance."

And so would I.

And so would Oscar.

And so I do.[29]

* * *

Despite being deeply moved by Tim's story, I placed the book on the bedside table and turned out the light. I had a full day of workshops and appointments planned for the morrow. Enough reading for tonight.

[29] Ibid., 23–29. Used by permission.

"The Call to Dance."

—Leahy, internationally acclaimed fiddling and step-dancing
family from Lakefield, Ontario.

(Watch the performance online:

https://www.youtube.com/watch?v=rqg0l43dbv4)

ten

THE CALL

What happened immediately after closing Huff's book was unexpected, unbidden—unbelievable! An exquisite zephyr. An intricate dance. Like a kite catching a warm, gentle current of air, I was filled by the breath of the Holy Spirit. He carried me upward, leading and guiding, sharing with me His wisdom and understanding (Isaiah 11:2), revealing the heart and will of the Father. This uplifting encounter, with its ethereal swirling sensation, was similar to that breath experience back in my attic bedroom so many years before. This time, however, I wasn't linked with the Triune God of the universe; as a woman in the church today, I was linked with Oscar, the boy with Down syndrome. And God reiterated the same message He presented at my first Write! Canada conference. Previously, He used Brian Stiller's story and the analogy of fence moving to make His point about women and the church, to reveal His troubled, dare I say broken, heart. This time around, His choice of symbolism was more creative, more complex; it involved the drama of the dance.

It was more inclusive as well. God is deeply grieved that all of His children aren't fully participating in this dance called life, and in particular that women aren't fully embraced by the life of the church. Although eager and excited to use our God-given gifts, we're frequently left on the periphery, like wallflowers waiting, wilting, at the annual spring dance. My Heavenly Father engaged the always mysterious, ever-empowering, out-of-the-box breath of His Spirit to enfold me in His embrace, to extend an invitation to the dance! Like Oscar, He's calling, not only me but *everyone*, to boogie to the beat, to plie to the pulse of His heart. "Dance while you can! Dance while you can!"

"Why are You showing me this?" I asked, flabbergasted by the force of it all, overwhelmed by its wonder. "What do You want me to do about it?"

"Write!"

"Right! I get it. That one little letter to the elders board didn't suffice. You want something better from me, something bigger, something bolder."

"A book," He impressed upon my heart.

I know the value of books, the power of that intimate exchange between writer and reader. For almost thirty years, I've worked as an author, publisher, and literacy advocate, and conducted hundreds, maybe over a thousand, classroom visits. Not to mention that from a young age I've been greatly influenced and inspired by my own reading. *Anne of Green Gables*, by Lucy Maud Montgomery, fostered a deep love of the natural world and a greater desire for scholastic achievement, as did *Girl of the Limberlost*, by Gene Stratton Porter. Best of all, these spunky female protagonists offered me a haven of unseen sisterhood in a home filled with noisy, rambunctious boys.

Gone with the Wind, read when I was much too young (pointed out by a friend of my mother who attended the Cobourg Alliance church), ignited a lifelong passion for history. And yes, I'll admit, romance, too. *The Adventures of Tom Sawyer*, by Mark Twain, and *Treasure Island*, by Robert Louis Stevenson, encouraged my thirst for adventure. Many of the above titles were safely stowed away in my Grandma Buttars' well-worn footstool. When Grandpa Buttars died, she moved in with my mother, her only child, and this hinged, leather hideaway accompanied her, becoming a cherished treasure chest to me.

Treasure-filled, too, are autobiographies and biographies of men and women of great faith. I make a point of reading a few every year, for they have significantly impacted my spiritual journey and continue to do so. As does the MVB, Most Valuable Book of all, the Holy Bible. I love to read and study its pages, always keeping in mind, as directed by A.W. Tozer, that the purpose of the written word is to direct us to the Living Word.

Indeed, we are shaped and moulded by the books we read. Every well-written book affects us in one way or another, seamlessly weaving itself into the fabric of our lives, becoming an integral part of who we are, whether we are aware of it or not.

> Books are the carriers of civilization. Without books, history is silent, literature dumb, science crippled, thought and speculation at a standstill. Without books, the development of civilization would have been impossible. They are the engines of change (as the poet said), windows on the world and lighthouses erected in the sea of time. They are companions, teachers, magicians, bankers of the treasures of the mind.[30]

The luminosity provided by the lighthouse in the above quote is reminiscent of the wisdom and guidance found in both Old Testament and New, as expressed in the theme verse from Pioneer Clubs, which I was involved in for so many years: *"Thy word is a lamp unto my feet, and a light unto my path"* (Psalm 119:105, KJV). I'll never forget the beautiful ballet dance performed by Jessica Melnik to accompany this verse at one of our Pioneer Club talent shows. It remains the most memorable outpouring of worship I've witnessed in a church setting, no doubt contributing to these words of the psalmist being treasured in my mind for all time.

N.T. Wright, former Bishop of Durham and one of the world's leading Bible scholars, sheds further light on the impact of reading God's Word:

> The Bible is breathed out by God (the word for "inspired" in this case is *theopneutos*—literally "God-breathed") so that it can fashion and form God's people to work in the world.

---

[30] Barbara W. Tuckman, *Goodreads*, "Quotable Quote." Accessed September 16, 2014 (www.goodreads.com/quotes/11087-books-are-the-carriers-of-civilization).

In other words, the Bible isn't there simply to be an accurate reference point for people who want to look things up and be sure they've got them right. It is there to equip God's people to carry forward his purposes of new covenant and new creation. It is there to enable people to work for justice, to sustain their spirituality as they do so, to create and enhance relationships at every level, and to produce that new creation which will have about it, something of the beauty of God himself…[31]

Our Abba Father, our Creator, desires that all His children play a unique and significant role in bringing this new creation into fruition.

The diligence of the Divine in pursuing the human soul and filling it with Kingdom purpose is described by English poet and homeless opium addict Francis Thompson (1859–1907), in his greatest work, "The Hound of Heaven." No doubt God was tired of hounding me. How foolish to think I'd given Him the slip on His writing assignment regarding women and the church. He's proven diligent in the pursuit of His purposes for my life. *"Many are the plans in a man's heart, but it is the Lord's purpose that prevails"* (Proverbs 19:21). I vowed to take more significant action on this issue. Yes, I would write a book (and with all deliberate speed). And yes, despite the fact that I, too, might be dancing with dynamite.

Books, indeed, are agents of change. And so is Spirit-empowered oratory. Grace Fox, international speaker, author, and co-director of International Messengers Canada (a missions ministry to Eastern Europe) spoke on Friday night. I had the great privilege of sitting next to her at lunch. N.J. Lindquist, award-winning author, editor, co-founder of The Word Guild, co-director of Write! Canada, and partner of That's Life! Communications, delivered the final plenary session on Saturday. N.J.'s passion is to see people fulfill their potential, becoming all God created them to be. Both of these messages further inspired, as did Denise Rumble, executive director of The Word Guild, who ascended the platform in order to close off the conference. God's presence permeated

---

[31] N.T. Wright, *Simply Christian: Why Christianity Makes Sense* (New York, NY: HarperCollins Publishers, 2006), 182–183.

the place, again confirming that He wants His daughters working and speaking on His behalf, and assuming leadership positions when called upon to do so.

The theme of this year's conference, "Change the World with Words," was reinforced in each of our minds as we left the auditorium with the soundtrack of Johnny Reid's "Today I'm Gonna Try and Change the World," playing in the background. How appropriate.

The aim and final end of all music should be none other than the glory of God and the refreshment of the soul.
—Johann Sebastian Bach,
organist and classical composer

eleven

LISTEN AND OBEY

There was only one major navigational decision to make as I drove along Highway 401 en route to my home in Peterborough after the conference: should I white-knuckle my way through the heart of Toronto on this formidable freeway, or take the access ramp near Halton Hills and link up with Highway 407, the more easygoing but expensive toll route? This seemed a mundane, unlofty thought compared to the others vying for space in my mind, for I was inspired, stoked by the synergy created by this gathering of diverse people with common passion and purpose. And I was determined to obey God more fully this time around. *"We must obey God rather than men"* (Acts 5:29b).

It's interesting to note that the Latin verb *obaudire*, meaning "to listen," is the origin of our English word "obedience." Quietness and stillness before God are essential for obedience, I've found, for how can we obey if our lives are too busy, too hectic to read His word, or if our surroundings are too noisy, too distracting, to listen for the soft, gentle whisper of His Spirit? Or, worst of all, if we let ourselves get so exhausted that we lack the energy to focus our minds on the very One who gave us breath (been there, done that, never gonna go back).

We need to listen and obey if we want to know God and experience Him in amazing ways. Whenever we make a conscious decision to obey God or not, we make an equally significant decision regarding our friendship, our intimacy with Him.

Whoever has my commands and obeys them, he is the one who loves me. He who loves me will be loved by my Father, and I too will love him and show myself to him. (John 14:21)

I wasn't about to risk losing any degree of divine intimacy or revelation by refusing to write this book.

Highway 407, I decided, swinging into the right lane and onto the exit ramp, despite the fact that this road is a behemoth rip-off compared to any other toll route I've travelled—literally highway robbery. A more relaxed drive would allow me to safely reflect on all I'd taken in the past three days: the intellectual stimulation, the wondrous praise, the new connections and friendships I'd made with incredibly talented people, the encouragement to write, and most importantly, the command to do so. Plus, I wanted to bounce a few questions off the One who issued the order—the God of the universe, the Omnipotent, Omnipresent, Omniscient One, not to formally request anything specific, per se, just to have a casual chat with my Creator.

"I wish I wasn't so technically impaired," I lamented.

No response from my life coach.

"What do you want me to do about it?"

My most competent, trustworthy writing mentor remained silent.

One of the panel discussions at the conference had dealt with utilizing social media for publicity purposes. Most publishers today, we learned, aren't interested in signing contracts with authors who lack a strong online presence. In other words, we need a professionally designed website with maximum SEO (Search Engine Optimization) and an active Facebook account with thousands of friends. Blogs are recommended, too, to help build a fanbase. We also need to be tweeting and retweeting (sounds a bit bird-brained to me, but then again, perhaps this is an insult to the birds) using consistent, effective hashtags, and so on and so on. One author, Sheila Wray Gregoire, suggested that to do a proper job, a writer needs to spend an hour and a half per day on the internet.

Yuck!

Yes, at some point, I supposed, I should become adept at this—develop a little social media savvy, so people will better know me and my books. But with my husband retiring, our plans for travel, and the need to renovate our newly acquired Armour Street home, not to mention everything else that was going on in our lives, I didn't even have much time for writing.

Once again, I directed my thoughts heavenward. "If I have any extra time right now, I think I'd rather be still and know You. I know You've called some people to dedicate their time to this kind of thing, and our new technology is taking Your Word further afield in amazing ways. (I think of Anne Voscamp and her Holy Experience blog inspiring thousands of readers a day.) But for me, right now, pursuing this would be a nuisance to knowing You. Don't You think?"

A strong sense of peace enveloped me and I felt God was in sync with my decision.

"But… by the way, what's this about?" I added. "This linking of women in the church with the boy with Down syndrome. I get the analogy of the dance and inviting women in the church to full participation. But comparing women to the boy with Down syndrome. Isn't that a bit much!"

I've nothing but respect for kids with Down syndrome. And for their parents and caregivers. One of my many nephews has the same chromosomal complexity as Oscar, the boy in the story. He too loves to dance, exuberantly. At family weddings, his shirt becomes soaked as he boogies to the beat in his "black boogie dogs." Josh's grin is contagious as he lives and loves life to the full.

"How am I like Josh?" I asked my Maker. "How am I like Oscar? How am I, as a woman in the church today, like these young men with Down syndrome?"

I was surprised by God's answer, but I got it. I've never forgotten it: "Marginalization."

"Marginalization," I mused, now back at home. I knew what the word meant, but even so, I checked out what my dictionary had to offer. My brow furrowed in thought as I read how the word applied to land. Basically, marginalized land is potentially fruitful ground that's underutilized until a shortage of more desirable land forces development. I smiled at the application for the church today.

In the months that followed, God brought this concept to the foreground in my own Bible study.

For thus saith the Lord to the men of Judah and Jerusalem, "Break up your fallow ground, and sow not among thorns." (Jeremiah 4:3, KJV)

I am concerned for you and will look on you with favour; you will be plowed and sown. (Ezekiel 36:9)

God desires to break up fallow ground and rain blessings upon all His children, empowering both men and women to fulfill their divine destiny. This will, in turn, produce fruit for His glory.

In reference to the original gouache painting reproduced on the cover of this book: "The Wood Thrush" seemed the perfect companion for this hymn and antique Gypsy violin. The harmonic qualities of this species at dawn combined with the rich colouring of its nape and breast are echoed in the violin... This piece is symbolic of the way God wants us to live—in unity and harmony with nature and with others as we "Rise to Greet the Sun" each new day.

—Kelly Dodge, artist, author, and naturalist

twelve

KNOWING GOD

I'll forever be in awe over what the Holy Spirit uttered that morning in my bedroom at our home on Armour Road.

"You know me," God said, these three simple words burrowing deep.

As mentioned in the opening chapter of the book, I was honoured and humbled by this experience, and I revelled in the fact that He assured me I'm the one to tackle this important project concerning His beloved daughters. I'd spoken on that same theme several times during the previous year—that women are God's beloved, daughters of the King, and followed that up at Auburn Bible Chapel in the spring with a presentation entitled "Rolling in the Deep," highlighting that Jesus, who bore the scars of God's love, is available to all of us today to heal our scars and woundedness. After making a few analogies to Adele's hit song, I outlined practical ways to draw closer to God, to develop greater intimacy, to sink deep in the soil of His love. Yet He clearly wanted me to take this theme to a more effective, more proactive level—to work toward loosening the chains of injustice and oppression that bind women in the church today.

Yikes!

I was fearful, too, for in the days following the conference I grasped the importance and magnitude of the mission and my own sense of unworthiness. I lost a bit of my resolve. Quite a bit! Thus, that early morning argument/discussion with God in Chapter One, which He brought to an abrupt halt with His stunning words of encouragement. "You know me."

The word "know" in Hebrew is *yada*. In our culture, "yada yada" signifies boring, empty talk. In Hebrew, *yada* is anything but boring. It can mean sexual intimacy, as a couple of my brothers and I discovered and giggled about while reading the Bible in church one Sunday morning when we should have been listening to the minister's sermon. Or it can mean to know passionately and intimately, not because of head knowledge, but through personal experience—to see for oneself. To deeply know the heart of another.

In the Old Testament, a select few people knew God intimately: prophets, priests, judges, kings, wise men, and a handful of charismatic leaders. Only the High Priest, after a great deal of cleansing, could go beyond the veil and enter the Holy of Holies, the innermost sanctum of the temple, in order to offer a blood sacrifice on behalf of the people. And this only once a year, on the Day of Atonement—Yom Kippur.

In the New Covenant, the one purchased by Jesus' blood, the one designed to rebuild, restore, and renew, all are invited into an intimate relationship with the Sovereign Lord of all the earth. Upon Jesus' death, the temple veil was torn, demonstrating that all are free to enter and enjoy God's holy presence. We can offer up a sacrifice of praise, move beyond the veil in prayer, fully rest in His unfathomable love, and feel the strong right arm of His embrace. We are encouraged to approach the unapproachable Yahweh, and relate to Him as Abba Father.

> *...since we have confidence to enter the Most Holy Place by the blood of Jesus, by a new and living way opened for us through the curtain, that is, his body, and since we have a great priest over the house of God, let us draw near to God with a sincere heart in full assurance of faith, having our hearts sprinkled to cleanse us from a guilty conscience and having our bodies washed with pure water. Let us hold unswervingly to the hope we profess, for he who promised is faithful. And let us consider how we may spur one another on toward love and good deeds.* (Hebrews 10:19–24)

The One who is most powerful, most fruitful at spurring Christians toward love and good deeds, is the Holy Spirit, for *"the fruit of the Spirit is love, joy, peace, patience, kindness, goodness, faithfulness, gentleness, and self-control"* (Galatians 5:22–23a). After Jesus' ascension, God's Spirit was sent to live in the hearts of all who would accept Jesus' gift of redemption and believe on His name (John 3:16). As Christians today, we are the tabernacle, the temple, the place where His glory dwells. God's Spirit, in turn, reveals to us the wisdom, the will, the heart of the Father. How exciting to think that we can intimately know our God!

According to A.W. Tozer, the greatest problem in making progress in our spiritual lives is our failure to give time to the cultivation of the knowledge of God. Tozer laments,

> Believing for salvation has these days been reduced to a once-done act that requires no further attention. The young believer becomes aware of an act performed rather than of a living Saviour to be followed and adored… Progress in the Christian life is exactly equal to the growing knowledge we gain of the Triune God in personal experience.[32]

Tozer informs us that what we think about God is the most important thing about us. He assures us, however, that God will always respond to our efforts to know Him.

This divine knowing involves a great paradox: the more we personally experience God, the greater will become our desire and pursuit, for deep calls unto deep. Saint John of the Cross says that Christ is

> like an abundant mine with many recesses of treasures, so that however deep individuals may go they never reach the end or bottom, but rather in every recess find new veins with new riches everywhere. (Spiritual Canticle 37.4).[33]

---

[32] A.W. Tozer, *The Root of the Righteous* (Harrisburg, PA: Christian Publications, Inc., 1955), 11.
[33] His Holiness John Paul II, *Crossing the Threshold of Hope* (New York, NY: Alfred A. Knoph, 1994), 128–129.

How wonderful that for as long as we live we can more greatly know and more deeply experience the God who is infinitely knowable.

Now we see but a poor reflection as in a mirror; then we shall see face to face. Now I know in part; then I shall know fully, even as I am fully known. (1 Corinthians 13:12)

Tozer offers us additional insight:

To know God is at once the easiest and the most difficult thing in the world. It is easy because the knowledge is not won by hard mental toil, but is something freely given. As sunlight falls free on the open field, so the knowledge of the holy God is a free gift to men who are open to receive it. But this knowledge is difficult because there are conditions to be met and the obstinate nature of fallen man does not take kindly to them.[34]

Knowing God doesn't mean we'll be free of temptations or trials in this life. The key to contentment, the Christian's secret to a happy life, is not the absence of troubles, but the presence of Jesus Christ in their midst.

I have told you these things, so that in me you may have peace. In this world you will have trouble. But take heart! I have overcome the world. (John 16:33)

In the midst of pain, if we choose to place our hand in the powerful, unfaltering grip of God, we'll come to know and understand more fully His comfort, love, faithfulness, mercy, and grace. In life's most difficult, darkest times, I've experienced God's most intimate revelations of Himself. This life experience, this *yada* knowing, has grown my faith and built my trust.

As part of a Bible study I developed several years ago, called Antiquarian Authors, I asked participants to take the title of a specific

---

[34] A.W. Tozer, *The Knowledge of the Holy* (New York, NY: Harper & Brothers, 1961), 122. A brief summary of these conditions is provided in the book's last chapter.

Frances Ridley Havergal poem ("They Say There Is a Hollow") and use it for inspiration in penning one of their own. John Piper says that "there are depths and heights and intensities and kinds of emotion that will not be satisfactorily expressed by mere prosaic forms, or even poetic readings. There are realities that demand to break out of prose into poetry and some demand that poetry be stretched into song."[35] This was the case with my poetic creation; I added the chorus of a familiar Havergal hymn ("Like a River Glorious") as the concluding stanza.

IN HIS HAND

They say there is a hollow
And I am graven there,
Etched upon the palm of God,
Forever in His care.

Through doubts and fears and trials,
He'll surely carry me.
When life's journey is complete,
His blessed face I'll see.

Stayed upon *Jehovah*
Hearts are fully blessed.
Finding as He *promised*
Perfect peace and rest.

Behold, I have graven thee upon the palms of my hands. (Isaiah 49:16a, KJV)

Yet I am always with you; you hold me by my right hand. You guide me with your counsel, and afterward you will take me into glory. (Psalm 73:23–24)

---

[35] Russ Hutto, *The Worship Community,* "Let's Sing & Make Melodies In Our Hearts To The Lord." Accessed: September 20, 2014 (www.theworshipcommunity.com/lets-sing-make-melodies-in-our-hearts-to-the-lord/). Quoting John Piper.

There's one more thing you should know. There are social justice connotations involved in the *yada*:

> *He did what was right and just… He defended the cause of the poor and needy, and so all went well. Is that not what it means to know me? declares the Lord.* (Jeremiah 22:15b–16)

Indeed, God has a heart for the poor and needy, as will we if we intimately know and love Him. But that same pulse beats just as compassionately for all who are oppressed (Isaiah 58:6). In the gospel accounts, we see how Jesus lived out the Father's heart by example, teaching His disciples to see and respond to the injustices that others ignored. The Holy Spirit is revealing that heart to me, and He will cause mine to more greatly resonate with His in the not too distant future.

I knew I'd eventually get to this God-given writing assignment about women and the church. I couldn't blatantly disobey, for I'd heard His voice loud and clear. I bought a notebook, a pink one (what was happening to me? I'd never bought anything pink in my entire life), and jotted down a few thoughts.

But alas, life got in the way. A season of busyness. And two moves within six months!

"Are you crazy?" our friends asked us.

No doubt.

A few months after settling in at Armour Road (four months after moving there, to be exact), immediately after I'd unpacked, washed, and put away the last box of dishware—that same evening, to be exact—my husband stumbled upon a newspaper flyer listing the sale of a home on the Otonabee River.

"We might want to check this out," he suggested. "Maybe we should buy a house on the river in a few years. Instead of moving north to one of the lakes, like we talked about. We'd be living right on the water, yet only five minutes from Home Depot." He smiled broadly, marvelling at the thought.

This, I now realize, is how many men must envision heaven.

"It won't hurt to start looking," I agreed. "It might take five years or so to find just the right spot."

We moved there six weeks later (November 2011) and spent the winter renovating the interior. My recently retired husband is handy with his hammer, and this new location on the beautiful Trent-Severn waterway, the meandering inland route between Lake Ontario and Georgian Bay had tremendous potential. And we were four to six minutes from Home Depot, depending on how we hit the traffic lights (to be exact).

We began the exterior restoration the following spring. We replaced the dented aluminum siding with board and batten; built a large deck across the front, with glass panels instead of railing so as not to hinder our beautiful view; erected a new garden shed and accompanying gardens; and of course added a good-sized dock for fishing, swimming, and boating. We worked tirelessly, transforming the property, and all the while I couldn't help but think about God and the work order He had given me—His restoration project on behalf of His beloved.

At the same time, I knew and acknowledged that finding this property was a gift from His hand. I was enthralled by the sound of silence the first night we slept here. Although within city limits and not far from Highway 115, this more southerly location was much quieter than Armour Road. My husband had also acquired an anti-snoring dental device, one that worked extremely well. Unbelievable, the improvement this made in my quality of sleep!

For the first time in my life, I had a proper office. No more kitchen table sprawled with papers and books and vintage teacups. No more Oompa Loompa room (my eldest son's nickname for my low-ceilinged, miniscule office in our basement on Weller Street, before the move to Armour Road). Here, on the river, I have an expansive, brightly lit, nicely furnished office of my own.

There's more: green space next door with a mix of mature deciduous and evergreen trees; tall, healthy cedar hedges providing privacy on both sides of our lot; and our own small beach area with easy-on-the-eyes, soft-on-the-sole entry to the water, perfect for future grandchildren. And the sunsets! We'd be staying here a good long time, Dave and I agreed.

Next came a season of celebration. We hosted my mother-in-law's ninety-fifth birthday party in June, with guests hailing from Montreal to Vancouver, then held an extended West family reunion in July. Most importantly, we prepared for our only daughter's wedding in late August. Hence the urgency for all that work in the spring.

But the Lord's purposes prevailed. Once the major preparations for the wedding were in place, I began waking in the night with snippets for the book flowing through my mind. Sometimes I would crawl out of bed, tiptoe to my office, and write them down. God was telling me: "Now is the time!"

Primarily, I was to record my personal experiences of how God had shown His heart to me regarding this issue. Yes, lots of *yada yada*.

"But what do You hope to accomplish with this book?" I asked in the hush of early morning, nothing disturbing communion with my Creator but the melodious refrain of birdsong.

"Harmony."

An admirer of his music once asked Leonard Bernstein what was the hardest instrument to play. "Second fiddle," he replied. "I can always get plenty of first violinists, but to find one who plays second violin with as much enthusiasm, or second French horn, or second flute, now that's a problem. And yet, if no one plays second, we have no harmony."

—Leonard Bernstein, world-renowned conductor

thirteen

HIS HEART FOR HARMONY

My friend Barbara and I scurried around the barn like mice, filling crown sealer jars and vintage glass bottles with stems of Queen Anne's lace, goldenrod, black-eyed Susans, Shasta daisies, and pretty petite sunflowers. Flanking these airy table centrepieces, functioning as candle holders, were the grey lids of crown sealers, beeswax tea lights placed within. On the head table, rusty gears showcased beeswax tapers, creating a more formal effect. Dainty jars of liquid honey, wedding favours previously placed on each ivory-draped table, picked up the golden hues veined in the barn boards and reflected the streams of light filtering through. We decided to position the bee-shaped sugar cookies later in the day. Laurie, another friend, had helped me bake and decorate two hundred of these and whole-wheat, hive-shaped cookies to accompany them. If we placed them on the plates beforehand, we just might return to discover the cookies gone and the resident mice licking their lips with satisfaction. The colours of my daughter Sarah's wedding were sunflower yellow and galvanized grey. This quaint rustic space came together better than any of us imagined.

Table-seating charts stood guard atop the stairs, at the entrance to the reception area—two aesthetically aged glass doors, with seating information written in white on each of the twenty-four panes. My daughter strategically placed smaller window frames about the barn etched with words of inspiration ("Candy Bar," "Love is Sweet").

Although the major theme of the wedding was "She's my Honey," the shabby chic decor conveyed another common thread which ran throughout the event—repurposing. It blended perfectly with the many antiques scattered about this peaceful pastoral setting, with the well-weathered covered bridge and pond side arbour.

Sarah carried the idea of repurposing right down to her wedding gown—1940's lingerie ordered online, transformed into an elegant dress with glitzy silver embellishments and intricate lace augmenting the bodice, as well as three tiers of aged lace added to the hem. The result was stunning.

"She looks like a Greek goddess," Barbara later informed.

Our daughter's wedding was a lot of work, but it was beautiful, too. Perfect weather, to boot. And speaking of, one of the highlights of the day was the foot-washing ceremony based on Jesus' example to His disciples (John 13:1–17).

For many years, traditional wedding ceremonies have included the word "obey." Those in contemporary Christian marriages, however, more readily choose to utilize meaningful expressions of mutual submission. After the exchange of vows and the proclamation of marriage, Pastor Peter Kenniphaas of Ferndale Bible Church introduced this symbolic segment of the ceremony:

> Clayton and Sarah feel deeply that they want their marriage commitment to reflect the principle of service. They want to serve one another, to place the needs of one another before their own. Jesus provided a powerful illustration of this principle when he washed the feet of His disciples. Jesus said, *"Now that I, your Lord and Teacher, have washed your feet, you also should wash one another's feet. I have set you an example that you should do as I have done for you"* (John 13:14–15). Clayton and Sarah are going to wash each other's feet as a symbol of their commitment to serve one another throughout their marriage.

Most of the wedding guests had never witnessed this physical demonstration of mutual submission, this act of servanthood, outlined in New Testament teachings (Philippians 2:3–4; Ephesians 5:21) and lived out by Jesus Christ (John 13:14), whose life provided the ultimate example. Sarah and Clayton's foot-washing ceremony, a symbol of sacrificial love, was a moving experience for us all. It, too, was in keeping with the overall theme of repurposing—a visual representation of the laying down of personal rights for the well-being of the other.

Mike Nappa, of Nappaland Communications, identifies five laws of servant living based on Jesus' example.

1. A faithful servant sees the need and meets it.
2. A faithful servant does the dirty work.
3. A faithful servant is determined to serve.
4. A faithful servant seeks no reward.
5. A faithful servant leads by example.[36]

Mutual submission isn't only good theology, but good psychology as well. According to Jack and Judith Balswick, recently retired marriage and family professors from Fuller Seminary and active family therapists:

> Assimilation in marriage, where the personhood of one spouse is given up, is not Christian... In Christian marriage each partner is subject to the other: each is to love and be loved, to forgive and be forgiven, to serve and be served, and know and be known. A marriage in which one partner, the husband or the wife, is asked to give up his or her personhood for the sake of the other denies God's expression in and through a unique member of the creation. The relationship is remarkably more fulfilling when both persons are equally expressed through their union.[37]

If one person continually makes sacrifices on behalf of the other and there's no reciprocity, intimacy suffers, as does fully knowing and

---

[36] Mike Nappa, *The Courage to Be Christian* (West Monroe, LA: Howard Publishing Co. Inc., 2001), 61–62.

[37] Jack and Judith Balswick, *The Family: A Christian Perspective on the Contemporary Home* (Grand Rapids, MI: Baker Academic, 1999), 85.

being known. Yet living out the concept of mutual submission in the real world is seldom a simple matter. There's constant shifting as partners adjust to one another, trying to find the balance, the rhythm, the give and take that works for their unique situation, eventually developing a pattern, an intricate dance, so to speak—ideally, one that flows in harmony with the music and tempo of their lives.

An admirer once asked world-renowned conductor Leonard Bernstein (1918–1990) what was the hardest instrument to play. Immediately, he replied,

> Second fiddle. I can always get plenty of first violinists, but to find one who plays second violin with as much enthusiasm, or second French horn, or second flute, now that's a problem. And yet if no one plays second, we have no harmony.[38]

In marriage, the willingness of both partners to play second fiddle is instrumental, contributing to harmony in the relationship and providing fitting accompaniment for the dance of intimacy. This is the ideal. At the very least, one partner must be willing to step up and play this instrument from time to time, providing harmony in the marriage (without being a doormat or subjecting themselves to an abusive situation, of course). If no one is willing to play second fiddle, discord will prevail. Knowing God is a key element in developing proficiency on this particular instrument, for God is love; knowing we are deeply loved frees us up to love one another.

I like how Mark Buchanan expresses this concept:

> Where does the courage to be servants even when it costs us something, maybe everything—where does that come from? It comes from knowing the love of God. And the more secure I am in God's love, the more free I am to be your servant... *Am I important?* Infinitely. *Do I matter?* Ultimately. *Am I loved?*

---

[38] Leonard Bernstein, *Gospel.com*, "Today's Devotional: Will You Play Second Fiddle?" Accessed: September 16, 2014 (http://www.gospel.com/blog/index.php/2010/03/16/todays-devotional-will-you-play-second-fiddle/).

Completely. So you know what? I don't have to sweat and fret about having a bigger slice of pie than you, a shinier nameplate on my door, more feathers in my cap, more notches in my gun stock, more letters after my name. I don't need anyone to pat me on the back and tell me how great I am. God's done all that and more. Now I'm free—to be your servant.[39]

At Clayton and Sarah's wedding, Pastor Peter said,

Love is the chief of all virtues, and it is this virtue, more than anything, that God wants to see expressed in your marriage. This verse, *"We love because He first loved us"* (1 John 4:19), makes it clear that your capacity to love is directly linked to your relationship with God. Coals that are close to the fire glow the brightest. Clayton and Sarah, I'd like to encourage you to continue to passionately pursue the Lord, both individually and together in your marriage so that the fire of His love will burn brightly in your lives.

Knowing God, it seems, has many positive repercussions, as does playing second fiddle. The two are tethered, contributing to freedom and intimacy in our relationships and enhancing our enjoyment of the dance called life.

Immediately after the wedding dance, Sarah and Clayton left for their honeymoon in New Orleans, just in time to meet up with Hurricane Isaac. My husband and I decided to take a honeymoon of our own. Dave had travelled extensively between high school and university, including a six-month sojourn on an Israeli kibbutz where he worked as a chicken farmer, but I'd never crossed the pond.

My Tuesday morning prayer group faithfully interceded on our behalf, asking God to help us find a good price on a Mediterranean cruise. When we visited CAA (Canadian Automobile Association) later that afternoon, the prices we were quoted were unbelievable. "Unheard

---

[39] Mark Buchanan, *Your God Is Too Safe* (Sisters, OR: Multnomah Publishers Inc., 2001), 215.

of," our agent remarked. Apparently, a sales flyer had been faxed to their office that very day.

We signed up for not one, but two cruises, which would bookend a brief stay in Rome. I should have been overjoyed, but I felt a little guilty. Shouldn't I be working on my book? Acting in obedience to God?

He'd been working on my behalf all along, I soon realized. We'd be going to many of the places the apostle Paul visited on his missionary journeys, including, on our second cruise, Turkey and the ancient city of Ephesus, the best-preserved classical city in the Eastern Mediterranean. This is where Paul directed much of his controversial material regarding women, women in marriage, and women in the church. He ministered to the Ephesian church over an extended time period—approximately fifteen years, even living in Ephesus for three years while on his third missionary journey (Acts 20:31). What an opportunity! I'd definitely have a better grasp of the cultural framework of Paul's writings once I'd walked the cobbled stones and marble promenades He walked upon, sat in the Great Theatre where he no doubt preached, touched the very columns he may have leaned against when wearied by his work. God's goodness knows no bounds!

My excitement peaked the night before the massive *Navigator of the Seas* was to dock in the port town of Kusadasi. Although once a prosperous seaport and an important commercial centre, because of the silting over of the Cayster River, Ephesus now enjoyed an inland location near the small modern town of Selcuk, approximately nine kilometres from the Aegean coast. We'd be travelling by bus to this impressive archaeological dig in Izmir Province early the next morning, where I hoped to unearth a bit of insight regarding Paul's directives to the church. Before I fell asleep that night, I prayed, "God can you show me why Paul instructed the women of the Ephesian church to be silent? (1 Timothy 2:11–12). It's totally opposite to what You're telling me."

"Harmony," He stated, matter-of-factly.

I was thrilled with His answer. With its simplicity. Its wisdom. This had been His exact response when I asked what He hoped to accomplish with this book promoting the full participation of women in the church today (keeping in mind a woman's giftedness and responsibility to family, the most important ministry of all, and ultimately, of course, her spiritual formation). In both scenarios, the underlying concept is the same—the desire for harmony in the church.

But we're dealing with two distinct time periods, two diverse cultural contexts, thus two very different approaches are required to achieve that common goal. Once again, I was amazed by my Maker—and by the fact that I'd be in this biblically significant setting the very next day!

What God is looking for to do his work on earth are second, third, and fourth fiddlers who are not seeking to glorify themselves, but to serve God by serving others, and thereby bring glory to God.

—Richard Innes, ACTS International

fourteen

ANCIENT EPHESUS

"Ephesus means 'hard-working bee,'" explained our hospitable, articulate guide when we began the forty-five-minute bus ride to the site of these extensive ruins. Immediately, I thought of my daughter's wedding, but soon my attention was captured by the clean, cosmopolitan nature of Kusadasi, our scenic port city: the restaurants, the shopping, the numerous resorts, the sandy beaches, and of course nearby Pigeon Island; Kusadasi means "Bird Island" in English, we were told. The panorama we beheld wasn't what we expected from Turkey.

As we made our way into the interior, this handsome, dark-haired forty-something-year-old pointed to an open area to our right.

"Used for camel wrestling," he informed. *Ahhs* all around the bus. "A female camel in heat is introduced to two male camels. Then the female is removed and the males battle it out." The bus grew quieter. We were intrigued. "They use neck leverage, or whatever means they can, until one runs scared or is brought to the ground."

I googled this traditional Anatolian spectator sport when I returned to Peterborough. It's a noisy event with boisterous fans, music, announcers, and the camels themselves—not so much their bellows, but the bells that adorn their colourful costumes. Their backs are draped with brightly coloured rugs and their intricate saddles are bead-embroidered and often fringed with pom-poms, and those clanging bells. The event is a sensory experience on all fronts, with barbeques and food stalls smoking, drums beating, flutes playing, families gathered in clusters for picnics, and camel handlers, as well as the camels themselves, jockeying for position. The winner of the dromedary duel (and its owner) receives a large sum of money, a beautiful hand-woven Turkish rug, or an equally valuable prize.

And the loser's fate?

"Camel sausage," our guide informed.

From the ceiling of the bus, he pulled down a small rolled-up map, an antiquarian sight in itself, and pointed out where we were headed. "In a few minutes you'll discover that Ephesus is located in a valley, surrounded by steep hills, offering protection from enemy attack. It was home to the Temple of Artemis, built around 550 B.C. One of the seven wonders of the ancient world. This temple was not only home to Artemis; it once housed four bronze statues of Amazon women. According to myth, they sought battle refuge here from Hercules."

I'd hoped to view the remains of this once-impressive temple, the Artemision, the place where the riot of the silversmiths of the "great" goddess Artemis had caused pandemonium (Acts 19:23–29), but it wasn't offered on the same shore excursion as the tour of Ephesus.

"Not a problem," said the young woman who worked the excursion desk of the cruise ship. "There's scarcely a trace of the temple left. Mmm… maybe a column or two. You're best to go to Ephesus." She gave a confident nod and friendly smile.

So much for the two-hour chant of "Great is Artemis of the Ephesians," recorded in Acts 19:28! The best-preserved columns of the Temple of Artemis are now in the British Museum in London, with a smaller sampling located in the Hagia Sophia, the sacred shrine of the goddess of wisdom, in Istanbul. Apparently, the temple was seriously damaged in a raid by the Goths in approximately 268 A.D. Today, only a single column remains.

During the classical Greek era, Ephesus was one of the twelve cities of the Ionian League. Wherever the Greeks settled, they worshiped the goddess Artemis, daughter of Zeus and Leto, twin sister of Apollo. This same goddess was revered by the Romans as Diana. In the Roman period (the first century B.C.), Ephesus' population reached more than

250,000, making it one of the largest cities in the Mediterranean world, the greatest trading city of Asia, hence a prominent religious centre. In the first century A.D., when Paul was active as a missionary here, Artemis of Ephesus was the deity worshipped by the entire civilized world. The goddess cult brought great economic prosperity to the city, the temple itself becoming the primary banking institution in Asia Minor.

A few quotes from *The Anchor Bible Dictionary* offer us insight into the confusing, ambivalent nature of the Artemis personality:

> Artemis the virgin huntress paradoxically contained within her personality obvious characteristics of a mother goddess... She zealously protects the suckling young of all wild animals, nurturing at their birth the very creatures she will later slaughter in the hunt... Fertility characteristics are strikingly apparent in her cult at Ephesus in Asia Minor: The Artemis whom the Ephesian mobs proclaim as "Great" at Acts 19:23–40 is a multi-mammary grotesque. In her capacity as mother goddess, Artemis was even the protectress of human children and was often identified with Eileithyia, the goddess-proper of human childbirth. The darker aspect of Artemis' personality is perhaps summed up and symbolized in her frequent identification with Hecate, a goddess of witchcraft and the moon who roves the night... The shedding of human blood was also an important component in the rites of Artemis Ortheia at Sparta; during these events, which became a tourist attraction in Roman times, youths were whipped until they bled... We may, at least to a point, account for the confusing multiplicity and ambivalence in Artemis' personality by regarding her as a humanized representation of untamed nature, which appears benign and life-giving at one time or place and cruel and destructive at another... Artemis is perhaps the most difficult of the Hellenic deities to comprehend and will undoubtedly always elude full explanation.[40]

---

[40] David Noel Freedman, ed., *The Anchor Bible Dictionary, Volume 1* (New York, NY: Doubleday, 1992), 464–465.

While touring the incredible, jaw-dropping Vatican museums a few days prior to arriving in Ephesus, I'd paid particular attention to the depictions of this Olympian goddess. Richard and Catherine Clark Kroeger, writing in *I Suffer Not a Woman: Rethinking 1 Timothy 2:11–15 in Light of Ancient Evidence*, describe this Asia Minor mother goddess in greater detail than I could ever hope to recall:

> She wore a high crown, modeled to represent the walls of the city of Ephesus; and her breastplate was covered with breast-like protuberances. Above these she wore a necklace of acorns, sometimes surrounded by the signs of the zodiac; for Artemis controlled the heavenly bodies of the universe. On the front of her stiff narrow skirt were rows of triplet animals, and on the sides bees and rosettes—an indication of her dominion over childbirth, animal life, and fertility... An elaborate system of magic developed upon the *Ephesia Grammata*, the six mystic words written on the cult statue of the goddess.[41]

Despite the male-dominated society of the Greeks in Asia Minor, the female was considered the primal source of all life. Although there were other mother goddesses (Cybele the mountain mother, for example), Artemis was most honoured within the city of Ephesus, which stood as a "bastion of feminine supremacy in religion"; in private devotion "she was the most worshipped of all the Gods."[42]

Much simpler and more pastoral in nature than the Ephesian mother goddess image is the Hellenistic huntress portrayal of Artemis. Carrying bow and arrows, crafted by Hephaestus and Cyclops, and wearing a flowing tunic, she frequently travelled the woods in the companionship of numerous mountain nymphs and her many dogs. As Dave and I walked these streets of antiquity, however, we were surprised that Ephesus was filled with cats. Lots of feline fur was curled up in crevices and corners, draped on stones and statues, and perched, purring softly, on the many

---

[41] Richard and Catherine Clark Kroeger, *I Suffer Not a Woman* (Grand Rapids, MI: Baker Book House Company, 1992), 53.

[42] Ibid., 52–54.

pillars that dotted the stony, uneven landscape. The dogs have dibs at the Acropolis in Athens, Greece, we had noticed at a previous port.

Navigating by foot, notebook in hand, we followed our guide's bouncing, bright orange umbrella as we meandered down gently sloping Curetes Street, named after the priests of Artemis. I was elated. I was keeping both of my beloveds happy; not only was I travelling with my husband, I was researching the book—working on my assignment from God. Once again, I was wonderstruck by how God works out all the details of our lives for His purposes.

My husband snapped photo after photo for me as we crisscrossed the centre of the complex in clusters: the civic agora, or public gathering place; the terrace houses depicting the lifestyle of the more affluent Romans; the men's latrine (with about twenty seats spaced rather closely together, with no partitions), a highlight for many in our group, based on their response; and the brothel, with its enticing signage, one of the first advertisements in all antiquity we were told.

At the base of the knoll, we finally reached the Celsus Library, one of the most impressive remains of all, its refurbished, sand-coloured facade backdropped in forest green and azure blue. Although not here in Paul's day—it was built in the second century—because of its amazing architecture this one-time home to over twelve thousand scrolls was exciting to view.

Two levels of columns towered above a raised platform of stairs leading to the three entrances of the building. Carved into one of these steps was an intriguing bit of ancient graffiti—a menorah, a prominent Jewish symbol, providing archaeological evidence of a Jewish community in Ephesus (Acts 19:8). At the top of the stairs, four spectacular female statues—symbolizing wisdom, faith, virtue, and knowledge—adorned the niches positioned across the front of the library, which also functioned as a monumental tomb for Roman Senator Tiberius Julius Celsus Polemaeanus. He lay beneath the interior ground floor, directly below a statue of Athena, Greek goddess of wisdom.

Mythology abounds here. So, too, ruins that pay homage to imperial religion and might. Buildings, monuments, and statues honour emperors, as well as the gods and goddesses of the ancient world.

From signage labelled "The 'Rhodian Peristyle' and the Prytaneum," where the city's sacred flame was kept:

The sacred quarter, probably built in the Augustan period (27 B.C.–A.D. 14), was dedicated to the deified Caesar and Goddess Roma or Artemis and Emperor Augustus.

The Prytaneum, erected in the same period, was entered via a courtyard (26 x 22m) surrounded by columns; this building was the office of the city's leading government dignitary. Its main room was used for public banquets for honoured individuals. The ashlar foundation in the centre of the room was either used as a sacred altar for Goddess Hestia, or a place for food preparation. In the area of the Prytaneum the four famous Roman copies of the statue of Artemis Ephesia were erected.

Indeed, in writing the pastoral epistles, Paul addressed a culture immersed in myth and magic, and one that utilized many intermediaries.

The cult personnel of the great temple of Artemis of Ephesus numbered into the thousands, some of whom certainly stood in an intermediary position between the deity and her worshippers... The priestesses passed through three ranks, the honeybees (or postulants), priestesses, and senior priestesses... By the first century C.E. the high priestess had replaced the high priest as the chief functionary of the cult, both at Ephesus and at neighboring Sardis.[43]

No wonder Paul was compelled to write, *"For there is one God and one mediator between God and men, the man Christ Jesus"* (1 Timothy 2:5).

While walking these newly excavated streets centuries later, Dave and I readily saw the influence of the feminine in Ephesus, not only in the signage posted throughout the ruins, but in the Artemis cult, and in much of the statuary and relief work, including one of Nike, goddess of

---

[43] Ibid., 70–71.

victory (goddess of the athletic shoe). I struck a pose with her, she with her winged arms stretched out gracefully, her one hand clutching what looks like a prized laurel wreath, me with my notebook and pencil.

The word *supernike* is found in the New Testament, in the phrase "more than conquerors," translated from the original Greek.

> *Who shall separate us from the love of Christ? Shall trouble or hardship or persecution or famine or nakedness or danger or sword? As it is written: "For your sake we face death all day long; we are considered as sheep to be slaughtered." No, in all these things we are more than conquerors through him who loved us. For I am convinced that neither death nor life, neither angels nor demons, neither the present nor the future, nor any powers, neither height nor depth, nor anything else in all creation, will be able to separate us from the love of God that is in Christ Jesus our Lord.* (Romans 8:35–39)

According to Paul, it is not the goddess Nike but Jesus Christ whose outstretched arms give the ultimate victory.

Paul is speaking from harsh experience here. He would have faced strong pagan resistance, not only in this place but on all his missionary journeys (1 Corinthians 16:8–9). Which begs the question: is Paul addressing heresy in his letter to Timothy regarding the Ephesian church, and not publishing *Church Practice 101* as many Christians have assumed?

> *I also want women to dress modestly, with decency and propriety, not with braided hair or gold or pearls or expensive clothes, but with good deeds, appropriate for women who profess to worship God. A woman should learn in quietness and full submission. I do not permit a woman to teach or to have authority over a man; she must be silent. For Adam was formed first, then Eve. And Adam was not the one deceived; it was the woman who was deceived and became a sinner.* (1 Timothy 2:9–14)

The women, once worshippers of the female-led Artemis cult, may have brought a great deal of her influence into the church, especially during times of childbirth. (If you're a woman who has given birth naturally, you will fully understand that last statement.) Maybe this is what Paul is referring to when he labels the Ephesian women as weak-willed (2 Timothy 3:6). He does warn Timothy against such influences: *"Have nothing to do with godless myths and old wives' tales; rather, train yourself to be godly"* (1 Timothy 4:7). And as far as instructions regarding physical appearance, they too could have been related to the goddess cult. Perhaps temple prostitutes wore braided hair and adorned themselves with jewellery. Or perhaps Paul is telling women not to mimic the ostentatious nature of the goddesses in their attire. Maybe he's simply advising them to avoid spending excessive money on frivolous fashion and boisterous bling, and to use it for good works, an underlying concept that could readily apply to Christians today. If Paul were writing to the modern church in southern Ontario, he might advise hockey fans not to shell out ridiculous amounts of money for Maple Leaf playoff seats, but rather use it for good deeds.

Gnosticism was also a threat to the early Christian church, with its blend of Greek and Oriental philosophy, intertwined with twisted Christian doctrine. Many Gnostic stories present Eve as pre-existing Adam. One story I encountered in my research involved Eve partnering with the serpent in the creation of the world. Satan is depicted as a malevolent benefactor and Eve as the source of spiritual awakening, the one who brings *gnosis*, or knowledge.

In light of all this false teaching, it becomes hard to determine how much of Paul's rationale restricting the women of Ephesus should be applied to women in the church today. No doubt a great deal was motivated by the need to address widespread heresy.

We may never fully comprehend all that was intended in this particular letter to this particular church at this particular time; we are all products of our own time—and place, I should add. When sitting in the company of Turkish people, I discovered, it's rude to expose the sole of your foot in the direction of another, something we pay no heed to in North America.

Not my feet, but my shoulders, gave me grief in Rome. Officially, it was in Vatican City State, the walled papal enclave within the city of Rome. It was extremely hot and sunny, and we had a full day planned: the Vatican, the Vatican museums, and later in the afternoon the catacombs. I'd opted to travel light—a sleeveless plaid top, with a high neckline and multi-layered ruffles on the bodice, and a black nylon skirt (not too short). And of course, sensible shoes and a wide-brimmed hat to keep the sun off my head and face.

After standing in a long line for a security check in order to enter the area, we queued up once again, this time for St. Peter's Basilica.

"Sorry, ma'am," the official gatekeeper of this world-renowned church and magnificent work of Renaissance art and architecture informed me. "You need to have your shoulders covered in order to come in here."

"What?"

"You need to have your shoulders covered, ma'am," he repeated. "Don't you have a scarf or something?"

I shook my head from side to side.

"Didn't you notice all the people selling them in the streets? You should have figured it out. Why do you think they were there? You'll have to go back outside and get one."

"Are you kidding? And stand in line all over again? We've just been on a cruise," I explained. "Every country, every port, had hundreds of people selling scarves. That didn't mean a thing to me. I've got five of them in my suitcase back at the hotel."

My husband chuckled at the irony of it all. "My wife's the most religious person I know," he said. "So, let me get this straight. You're letting me in the church… and you're kicking her out." He shot a smug smile in my direction.

The guard was not amused.

Neither was I. I launched a verbal barrage. "There should have been a sign or something. Or one of the security guards at the main entrance should have brought this to my attention. I really should have done a bit of research before coming here, I know, but this was a last-minute trip, and it didn't seem to matter in any of the other countries we visited.

Don't you have a couple of scarves or something for people who aren't aware of the rule, or who forget." I gazed up at his imposingly large form with pleading eyes. "Couldn't you just let me take a quick peek inside?"

He shook his head while I watched a women with excessive cleavage enter the Basilica.

"I'm not trying to be disrespectful," I said. "I just don't want to have to stand in line all over again."

"Sorry, ma'am," he repeated, his voice growing firmer as another buxom bosom billowed by.

Apparently, partially exposed breasts were fine, but bare shoulders were taboo. Who knew? Everyone but me, it seemed.

I was extremely frustrated at this point, becoming desperate, more creative. "What if I hang my big straw hat off my left shoulder and hold my purse over my right one? Would that work?"

He wasn't buying any of this and my husband was getting a little worked up. "This is stupid," Dave said. "This is a church. I thought churches were supposed to want people to come in."

"It's okay," I said, finally giving up, shrugging the offensive shoulders and waving Dave on. "You go in. I'll just wait for you outside." I calmed myself down by quoting scripture in my head: *The Lord does not look at the things man looks at. Man looks at the outward appearance, but the Lord looks at the heart"* (1 Samuel 16:7b).

Someday, I told myself, *this will make a great illustration to go along with this verse. And wait until I get home and tell my oldest son, who recently informed me I was getting "old lady arms," that these "old lady arms" were too sexy for St. Peter's Basilica.*

The best was yet to come.

"You have to see inside," Dave announced after joining me once again. "You may never get another chance. And you won't ever need to see another basilica after you've seen this one. It's amazing!" He pulled me behind a massive pillar and yanked his T-shirt over his head. "Here, put this on."

My mouth dropped open at his unexpected boldness. "Aren't *you* breaking some kind of dress code?"

I scanned the area, but no one was watching us, so I quickly pulled it on and walked briskly past the security guard, who took no notice. I spent a few minutes marvelling at the interior: the beauty, the vastness, and the incredible works of art, including Michelangelo's marble *Pieta*, the famous sculpture of Mary holding Jesus on her lap immediately after His crucifixion. Indeed, the Basilica was, as Ralph Waldo Emerson aptly described, "an ornament of the earth... the sublime of the beautiful."[44]

Yet I couldn't linger and fully savour the experience. I was haunted by the thought of bailing Dave out of an Italian jail for indecent exposure at the Vatican. Friends and family back home in Peterborough might end up watching him being arrested on the six o'clock news. I quickly exited the building and found my husband, peering out from behind his pillar.

"It wasn't so bad," he explained. "A few frowns. One angry man pointed his finger and yelled something I didn't understand. But it would have been a shame for you to miss it."

Later, once we'd descended the stairs and joined the other tourists gathered below in St. Peter's Square, we realized that hundreds of people must have observed our actions. Those who missed seeing Dave pass his shirt over to me would have wondered why this brazen, bare-chested man was hiding behind one of the columns of St. Peter's Basilica. I vowed that I would do more research before our next trip.

More recently, I learned of another cross-cultural contrast while chatting with a Ugandan friend. We were talking about some of the cultural misunderstandings that occur when North American missionaries minister alongside national workers.

"In my country," Lydia Teera explained, "if you look people in the eye when you talk to them, it shows a lack of respect. This is especially true when speaking with the elderly."

It's just the opposite here in Canada, providing further evidence that we need to understand the subtle nuances of New Testament culture before we can make sweeping generalizations regarding how Paul's instructions to the early church in Asia Minor apply to us today. Unfortunately, this may prove impossible. That's why it's important to not only read the Word of God but rely on the work of the Holy Spirit,

---

[44] Susan, *Vatican Art Historian*, "Saint Peters Basilica." Accessed: September 20, 2014 (http://vaticanarthistoriantours.com/2011/01/saint-peters-basilica/).

the One who knows the heart and mind of God firsthand, and welcomes the opportunity to share that knowledge with us.

One thing Bible scholars do know is that

> *hesychia*, translated "quietness" in 1 Timothy 2:11 and "silent" in verse 12, doesn't mean complete silence or no talking. It is clearly used elsewhere (Acts 22:2; 2 Thess. 3:12) to mean "settled down, undisturbed, not unruly."[45]

It can also mean peace or harmony (1 Timothy 2:2). A different word (*sigao*) means "to be silent, to say nothing" (Luke 18:39; 1 Corinthians 14:34).[46] The Corinthian passage states that

> *women should remain silent in the churches. They are not allowed to speak, but must be in submission, as the Law says. If they want to inquire about something, they should ask their own husbands at home; for it is disgraceful for a woman to speak in the church.* (1 Corinthians 14:34–35)

The issue of women's silence in the Corinthian church is one of the topics N.T. Wright addressed in his conference paper for the symposium "Men, Women and the Church," held at St. John's Conference in Durham, England on September 4, 2004:

> I have always been attracted… to the explanation offered once more by Ken Bailey. In the Middle East, he says, it was taken for granted that men and women would sit apart in church, as still happens today in some circles. Equally important, the service would be held (in Lebanon, say, or Syria, or Egypt), in formal or classical Arabic, which the men would all know but which many of the women would not… one of the things you learn in real pastoral work as opposed to ivory tower academic theorizing is

---

[45] John Walvoord and Roy Zuck, eds., *The Bible Knowledge Commentary: An Exposition of the Scriptures by Dallas Seminary Faculty* (Wheaton, IL: Victor Books, 1983), 735.
[46] Ibid.

that you simply can't take a community all the way from where it currently is to where you would ideally like it to be in a single flying leap. Anyway, the result would be that during the sermon in particular, the women, not understanding what was going on, would begin to get bored and talk among themselves... the level of talking from the women's side would steadily rise in volume, until the minister would have to say loudly, 'Will the women please be quiet!', whereupon the talking would die down, but only for a few minutes. Then, at some point, the minister would again have to ask the women to be quiet; and he would often add that if they wanted to know what was being said, they should ask their husbands to explain it to them when they got home. I know there are other explanations... this is the one that has struck me for many years as having the strongest claim to provide a context for understanding what Paul is saying. After all, his central concern in 1 Corinthians 14 is for order and decency in the church's worship. This would fit extremely well.[47]

This brings us to the problem with much of Paul's writing regarding women: not everything fits. There are inconsistencies. Sometimes he tells women to be silent in the church (1 Timothy 2:12; 1 Corinthians 14:34), while on other occasions he instructs them how to speak and prophesy:

Every man who prays or prophesies with his head covered dishonors his head. And every woman who prays or prophesies with her head uncovered dishonors her head—it is just as though her head were shaved. (1 Corinthians 11:4–5)

There are inconsistencies in the way the church has handled these biblical passages as well. The 1 Timothy 2 verses quoted previously pertaining to women are preceded by a directive to men regarding their

[47] N.T. Wright, *Women's Service in the Church: The Biblical Basis,* a conference paper for the Symposium, "Men, Women and the Church." St. John's College, Durham, September 4, 2004.

behaviour in church: *"I want men everywhere to lift up holy hands in prayer, without anger or disputing"* (1 Timothy 2:8). I never saw our men lifting their hands in prayer while the women remained silent. How can a church randomly pick and choose which verses apply today and which do not? I sense the inclusion of the phrase *"without anger or disputing"* indicates that a specific problem is being addressed here. There seems to be a male problem of anger and a female problem of disruptive verbal behaviour in the church at Ephesus. Paul is advising Timothy, his son in the faith, how to handle these issues.

Tonight, as I write, my oldest son, a high school teacher, is writing his report cards. Immediately after talking to him on the phone, the Holy Spirit directed, "Think of your own reports." Suddenly, I made a connection between my report cards and Paul's instructions to the women of Ephesus. My grades were always great, and I was well-liked by my teachers, but they always commented on my talkative nature. "Stop talking in class," they would write. Or "Please keep quiet." This didn't mean I should never talk at school again. It simply drew attention to a personality problem I was bringing into the classroom. To a shy, reluctant girl, this same teacher might have written, "Speak up more often." Did Paul admonish the women of the Ephesian church in the same manner? He certainly didn't mean that women in the church were to be literally mummed for millennia.

> *In the last days, God says, I will pour out my Spirit on all people. Your sons and daughters will prophesy, your young men will see visions, your old men will dream dreams. Even on my servants, both men and women, I will pour out my Spirit in those days, and they will prophesy.* (Acts 2:17–18)

This passage is important, for it appears in both the Old Testament (Joel 2:28–29) and the New. It underlines the fact that before we can make significant theological conclusions, we need to look at the whole body of Scripture.

The late L.E. Maxwell, previously president of Prairie Bible Institute, once declared that more than a hundred passages of scripture "affirm women in roles of leadership, and fewer than half a dozen appear to be in opposition."[48] Consider Deborah, prophetess and judge (Judges 4:4); Huldah, court prophetess (2 Kings 22:14–20); Junia, who was *"outstanding among the apostles"* (Romans 16:7); Priscilla, teacher and church planter (Romans 16:3–5); Phoebe, a deacon (Romans 16:1–2); and Mary, mother of our Lord (Luke 1:26–55), lest we forget that motherhood is the most influential role of all.

Upon a careful study of New Testament scripture, Gilbert Bilezikian, author of *Community 101: Reclaiming the Local Church as a Community of Oneness*, identifies two types of New Testament churches he feels are biblically legitimate (and at the same time accounts for what may seem at a superficial reading to be an inconsistency on Paul's part). One model he calls "normative," while the other he terms "remedial." The latter classification, he believes, applies to the church at Ephesus.

According to Paul, many of the women in the Ephesian church were unstable and double-minded. Paul writes about *"weak-willed women, who are loaded down with sins and are swayed by all kinds of evil desires, always learning but never able to acknowledge the truth"* (2 Timothy 3:6-7).

Belizikian writes:

> The excesses that caused the Ephesian women's temporary removal from the teaching ministry illustrate how easily the use of authority can be turned into abuse. Such abuse occurs readily when hierarchial structures are allowed to replace networks of servanthood as the infrastructure of community, and when recourse to authority becomes the norm in Christian relations instead of being held in reserve as a remedial resource, to be utilized mainly for cases of emergency and prevention.[49]

The normal mode of function for a healthy New Testament church involves empowering the totality of the church with servant leadership

---

[48] Richard and Catherine Clark Kroeger, *I Suffer Not a Woman* (Grand Rapids, MI: Baker Book House Company, 1992), 33.

[49] Gilbert Bilezikian, *Community 101, Reclaiming the Local Church as a Community of Oneness* (Grand Rapids, MI: Zondervan Publishing House, 1997), 153.

(2 Corinthians 4:5), in partnership with the Holy Spirit, who supplies a diversity of gifts, as well as the power and wisdom for appropriate application (1 Corinthians 12). The analogy of the body, with Christ as the head, which Paul readily promotes (Ephesians 1:22–23; Romans 12:4–21; 1 Corinthians 12), provides a fitting picture of God's preferred *modus operandi.*

Paul advised the church in Ephesus to move beyond their immaturity:

Then we will no longer be infants, tossed back and forth by the waves, and blown here and there by every wind of teaching and by the cunning and craftiness of men in their deceitful scheming. Instead, speaking the truth in love, we will in all things grow up into him who is the Head, that is Christ. From him the whole body, joined and held together by every supporting ligament, grows and builds itself up in love, as each part does its work. (Ephesians 4:14–16)

Sounds like each and every one of us is called to play second fiddle, not only in our marriage relationships but in the church. Christ is to play first fiddle, and we are instructed by God to harmonize.

And God placed all things under his feet and appointed him to be head over everything for the church, which is his body, the fullness of him who fills everything in every way. (Ephesians 1:22–23)

It was he who gave some to be apostles, some to be prophets, some to be evangelists, and some to be pastors and teachers, to prepare God's people for works of service, so that the body of Christ may be built up until we all reach unity in the faith and in the knowledge of the Son of God and become mature, attaining to the whole measure of the fullness of Christ. (Ephesians 4:11–13)

I love God's brilliantly simple response to the question of women and the church. Bottom line: He desires harmony. Just as restricting the women of Ephesus in Paul's day would have achieved this result, encouraging women to function within the norms of twenty-first-century culture will bring greater harmony today. The result will be Kingdom good if we approach the issue with love, mutual respect, and humility. If we value, develop, and utilize the Holy Spirit's distribution of giftedness. If we model Jesus' servant leadership style and seek the wisdom and will of the Father.

It's time to move on.

I am a fiddler. I desire it. I breathe it. I play it.
Whether I play on stage or in the kitchen for my kids,
I'm a fiddler.

—Natalie MacMaster, master fiddler

fifteen

THE GREAT THEATRE

Tucked snugly in the slope of Panayir Hill, just beyond the ceremonial gates honouring Caesar Augustus, is the largest, most impressive site in all of Ephesus—the Great Theatre. Built by the Greeks in the third century B.C., both enlarged (41–54 A.D.) and completed by the Romans in the early second century A.D., this amphitheatre boasts phenomenal acoustics and seating for twenty-five thousand spectators. Although no longer playing host to major public concerts because of potential damage to the site, Sting, Pavarotti, and Elton John all performed here.

"Take fifteen minutes to explore the theatre," our guide suggested after giving the group a quick lesson on identifying the various columns of antiquity. Tall and sentinel-like, Ionic, Corinthian, and Composite columns lined the processional promenade bordering the entrance to the theatre, although once extending all the way to the Temple of Artemis approximately three kilometres away.

The psalmist David compared God's daughters to these beautiful architectural structures: *"Our daughters will be like pillars carved to adorn a palace"* (Psalm 144:12b). This figurative language points to beauty and substance working together to achieve a goal, function and form in complete harmony.

This particular daughter of the Most High God broke into a jog on the marble promenade in order to make maximum use of the time available. I wasn't so much interested in the architectural details of the columns, although they were impressive; I wanted to enter and experience the expansiveness of this amphitheatre, sit on one of the massive slabs of stone step-lining the interior, and breathe in the atmosphere, envisioning all that would have taken place in this ancient space.

The Romans enlarged the stage area, as well as the seating capacity, in order to host not only celebrations honouring Artemis, concerts and plays, and religious and philosophical debates, but to provide a suitable venue for more thrilling entertainment such as exotic wild beast shows and gruelling gladiatorial combat. We know, without a doubt, that gladiators fought and died in ancient Ephesus; there is a gladiator graveyard nearby.

Although we have no historical evidence, tradition tells us, as did our guide, that Paul preached here. According to the book of Acts, however, after speaking boldly in the synagogue for a three-month period, much of his healing and teaching ministry took place in the lecture hall of Tyrannus (Acts 19:8–11). Even so, it does seem fitting that at some point in his ministry Paul addressed the people from the stage of the Great Theatre, the centre for religious discourse and debate.

The Bible does offer details regarding an incident concerning Paul:

> *A silversmith named Demetrius, who made silver shrines of Artemis, brought in no little business for the craftsmen. He called them together, along with the workmen in related trades, and said: "Men, you know we receive a good income from this business. And you see and hear how this fellow Paul has convinced and led astray large numbers of people here in Ephesus and in practically the whole province of Asia. He says that man-made gods are no gods at all. There is danger not only that our trade will lose its good name, but also that the temple of the great goddess Artemis will be discredited, and the goddess herself, who is worshipped throughout the province of Asia and the world, will be robbed of her divine majesty." When they heard this, they were furious and began shouting: "Great is Artemis of the Ephesians!" Soon the whole city was in an uproar. The people seized Gaius and Aristarchus, Paul's*

travelling companions from Macedonia, and rushed as one man into the theater. Paul wanted to appear before the crowd, but the disciples would not let him. (Acts 19:24–30)

Fortunately, the city clerk brought the crowds under control (Acts 19:35–41).

Approximately two thousand years later, the awe-inspiring amphitheatre of Ephesus is still drawing crowds. According to the man wielding the orange umbrella, fifteen thousand people toured this ancient site the day before we arrived, most visiting the city via the massive cruise ships docked in the port of Kusadasi.

I figured that at some point, Paul must have prayed in this Great Theatre, for it was the most significant gathering place in the social and cultural life of Ephesus. Perhaps he circumnavigated the amphitheatre on foot, praying for the salvation of the people gathered within. I sat on a large grey stone and asked for wisdom and guidance for the important writing project I would undertake when I returned home. I didn't address my petition to Athena, the Greek goddess of wisdom and war who stood in the library above the tomb of Celsus, nor to Sophia, the Roman goddess of wisdom who was securely ensconced in one of the niches that adorned the library's impressive facade. I spoke to the one true God of the universe, He who is sovereign Lord of all Creation, the One in whom, according to Paul, *"we live and move and have our being"* (Acts 17:28).

At home in Peterborough, on my writing desk, sits a small grey stone artfully etched with a single word—wisdom. This tiny rock enjoys a strategic location immediately to the left of my computer screen and directly in front of my portable phone, in order to remind me to seek the Holy Spirit's wisdom in all I write or say throughout the day. Theologically speaking, it's an *Ebenezer.*

The word *Ebenezer* is Hebrew, meaning "stone of help." *Even* meaning "stone," and *ezer* translating as "help."

Then Samuel took a stone and set it up between Mizpah and Shen. He named it Ebenezer, saying, "Thus far has the Lord helped us." (1 Samuel 7:12)

This Hebrew word is found in the original version of the hymn "Come Thou Fount of Every Blessing":

> Here I raise my Ebenezer,
> Hither by thy help I've come.

The church has modernized this verse to read,

> Hitherto Thy love has blest me,
> Thou has bro't me to this place.

Some modernizations are helpful, while others may hinder, for in so doing we've lost a reference to a profitable, biblically inspired practice. The initial wording of this hymn causes contemporary Christians to question and leads us to the Bible, not a bad place to be bro't. In addition, as a writer, I have empathy for the original author, Robert Robinson (1735–1790), who was only twenty-two when he penned these lines lauding the amazing gift of divine grace. How long did he labour over that one line, hoping to find just the right word to express his thoughts? Perhaps the Holy Spirit gifted him with the word *Ebenezer.*

Of particular interest to us is that the word *ezer* (help) in the 1 Samuel passage is the same word used to describe Eve in Genesis 2. According to biblical scholars, this word is never used of a subordinate.

> Of its twenty appearances in the Old Testament (in addition to the Genesis reference), seventeen are references to God as our helper. (The other three refer to a military ally.)[50]

Despite its etymology, an *Ebenezer* need not be a stone. Anything that reminds us of God's love, His presence and power, can function as an *Ebenezer*. A cranial colander at the best of times, my middle-aged brain needs visual prompts to help keep me focused. I've planted a few *Ebenezers* around my home and garden to refocus my attention on the

---

[50] Stanley J. Grenz and Denise Muir Kjesbo, *Women in the Church* (Downers Grove, IL: InterVarsity Press, 1995),164. See Psalm 10:14, Psalm 70:5, and Deuteronomy 33:29.

Divine, and to create a constant reminder of His work in my life: an encouraging fridge magnet in a pivotal spot in the kitchen; a "Be Still and Know" print near my bedside; a Honeybells Hosta by my front door, a reminder of the time God called me honey; a Gentle Shepherd daylily in the garden, amidst a meandering drift of Lamb's Ears, a subtle testimonial to the fact that our Lord is just that—winsomely wooing, tenderly guiding, and gently prodding us to pursue His purpose for our lives.

The small stone on my writing desk, with six tiny letters beautifully engraved in gold, functions as an *Ebenezer*, reminding me to daily seek God's wisdom. This particular *Ebenezer* is literally a stone of help.

Choose my instruction instead of silver, knowledge rather than choice gold, for wisdom is more precious than rubies, and nothing you desire can compare with her. (Proverbs 8:10–11)

While writing an Old Testament Bible study a few years ago, I came to realize that through the power of the Holy Spirit, God offers each of us the same wisdom He offered King Solomon. Incredible! If any of us lack wisdom, we can *"ask God, who gives generously to all without finding fault"* (James 1:5). Paul asked for this gift on behalf of the saints in Ephesus:

I keep asking that the God of our Lord Jesus Christ, the glorious Father, may give you the Spirit of wisdom and revelation, so that you may know him better. (Ephesians 1:17)

I pray this verse not only for myself, but on behalf of each and every one of you today.

I pray also that the eyes of your heart may be enlightened in order that you may know the hope to which he has called you, the riches of his glorious inheritance in the saints, and his incomparably great power for us who believe. (Ephesians 1:18–19a)

The eyes of both my heart and mind have been enlightened after physically experiencing ancient Ephesus. I've not only acquired valuable insight into the writings of Paul, I've gained firsthand evidence of the authenticity of the Word of God. While walking these marble promenades, one can readily imagine the craftsmen selling their Artemision wares in the commercial agora, the main marketplace of the city, as well as the agitated crowds rushing toward the theatre which stood nearby.

My husband and I exited the theatre and passed by the gladiator graveyard on our way to meet up with our guide. We paused for a moment to watch a brief costumed re-enactment of Ephesian life during Roman times, then wandered through the cluster of local artisans strategically located near the tour bus parking lot. Today, craftsmen, *as well as craftswomen*, ply their trade.

While fiddling, don't Bb or B#, just B natural...
—Anonymous

sixteen

THE ARENA OF LIFE

Our travel agent's information was a little ambiguous at this point of the trip. After we disembarked the *Navigator of the Seas* in the small Italian port town of Civitavecchia, we weren't sure if we were to meet our shuttle service at 9:00 or 10:00 a.m. Best to play it safe, we decided.

Perched on my large, overstuffed, lime green and black duffle bag, I ended up observing the comings and goings at the cruise terminal for over an hour. Several drivers met their anxious passengers, swung large suitcases into available storage space, filled their buses, and sped off to the airport in Rome about fifty kilometres away. My mind was also scrambling, running here and there on possible trails and tangents, hopping on board even the most tenuous train of thought, or flying off on innumerable flights of fancy, as is its tendency when contemplating the writing of a new book.

Mmmm… should all church ministry positions be open to women? I wondered. I felt this was what God had been telling me of late, but as I watched the bus drivers, all men, manhandle the mounds of heavy luggage, I began to think that perhaps there were some jobs women shouldn't attempt to do. Immediately after this thought, I spotted our bus pulling into the parking lot and jumped to my feet. A couple dozen of us stood, eyes wide, mouths agape, luggage in hand, as a beautiful, tall, strong blonde women about thirty-five years old descended the small flight of stairs and warmly greeted us.

Is this how the ancients envisioned the Amazons? I wondered as she womanhandled our bags with ease. And with more care than most of the male drivers, I should add. Her driving proved impeccable. Her demeanour was charming and she seemed to really enjoy her job. My gender generalizations flew straight out the bus window.

Don't get me wrong. In no way am I saying that men and women are the same. I've done the Bible studies, read the books (*Men Are from Mars, Women Are from Venus*). I've lived long enough to know better. I'm not promoting abandoning the distinctions of gender, but rather redeeming them. The very fact that men and women are different is one of the key reasons the church needs to embrace the partnership of women. Differing perspectives and a wider skillset can only enhance the function of the church. That bus driver was using her God-given gifts and talents in ways that were in sync with her physical abilities and intrinsic personality. The result was a harmonious experience for us all.

Shouldn't the church get to experience the full potential and giftedness of its women as well? Was the sacrifice of Christ powerful enough to cover all my sins and remove them *"as far as the east is from the west"* (Psalm 103:12) but not potent enough to handle that one sin of Eve? Will that Tertullian title, "the devil's gateway," always apply to us women? The song says, "There is power in the name of Jesus to break every chain."[51] I'm assuming that includes those imposed in Genesis 3. Indeed, how can an apple trump the blood of Jesus?

Yet common sense must prevail both in the church and in society at large. My husband recently observed two female paramedics, both slight of frame, answer an ambulance call to attend a large man. They struggled to load him on the gurney, no doubt creating an uncomfortable scenario for everyone involved—a nonsensical scenario as far as we were concerned.

Our vacation was truly incredible, full of enough Mediterranean memories to last a lifetime, but the return flight was difficult for me, with my restless legs and antsy personality. I walked the aisles and went

---

[51] Will Reagan, "Break Every Chain," United Pursuit Records, 2009.

for countless bathroom breaks in order to stretch my muscles and retain my sanity. Back at home, I experienced the annoyance of severe jetlag; it took a couple of weeks for my energy level to return to normal. My spirits were lifted, however, upon the arrival of our local courier carting a small cardboard box.

Several months before our trip, the editors of *Chicken Soup for the Soul* had emailed, asking me to consider submitting a story for their upcoming "Hooked on Hockey" book.[52] I wasn't that worried about it, although they did pay two hundred dollars and ship me ten free copies. At the time, I felt that if I had any extra writing time, I should be writing "The Book." Even so, I felt God nudging me to document an experience from my early childhood and submit a story. Not only a story about hockey, Canada's beloved national winter sport, but one based on my feelings regarding gender exclusion.

THE ARENA OF LIFE

Hockey, people say, is what defines us as Canadians. I don't know if I totally agree. Granted, the game's image has been copied onto our currency, but we are a more diverse lot than that. I have to admit, however, that hockey did play a defining role in my life back in the 1960s.

As young children, it was pond hockey that my brothers and I enjoyed. A similar scene is enshrined on the back of Canada's five-dollar bill, in a painting entitled "The Pond." Two such surfaces lay within walking distance of our childhood home. Nestled amidst the rolling hills of Northumberland County, these frozen platters offered considerable protection against the bitter winds of winter, while we played the game we learned to love. One pond even came with its own warming hut—an ancient, abandoned, navy blue Chevy. Bereft of windows and doors, stripped of its motor and wheels, the car had been dragged to the marshy water's edge in order to function as a duck blind for a group of hunters in the mid-forties. It provided the perfect place to sit and chat while we laced up our skates… mine, the lone white pair among all the black and brown ones.

---

[52] I had a hockey story previously published in their "O Canada" edition.

There was plenty of pleasure to be found playing pond hockey:

- The ethereal beauty of a wintery landscape when robed in ice and snow.
- The camaraderie created as we shovelled off the snow-covered ice.
- The sheer joy of making up our own rules, with no adults around to enforce theirs.
- The serene quiet of the outdoors as a backdrop to the pleasing clicketty-clack of stick on ice.
- The ecstatic feeling of freedom as we raced over the ice, cool, crisp air rushing over ever-reddening faces.
- The clean, clear smack of the puck on a perfectly executed give-and-go.
- The euphoric invigoration of strenuous outdoor exercise and the blissful sleep that followed later that night.
- And occasionally, the glorious magic of pristine, clear ice when a flash freeze followed a January thaw.

Of course, we experienced our fair share of frostbitten fingers and toes, the odd unintentional clip to the head or other minor injury, the sight of blood on snow, but all this paled in comparison to the delight offered by puck on pond. Cast-off boots became goaltender pipes, the sun overhead the time clock, snow banks the boards.

In mid-winter, our one-room schoolhouse offered more of the same icy enchantment. On Friday afternoons, we experienced physical education at its finest. With sticks and skates slung over our shoulders, we often walked with our teacher to a nearby farmer's field for a game of shinny.

And then, the inevitable—change. Mulholland's School (S.S. #11) closed and my brothers and I transferred to the one in the nearby village of Baltimore. This was nothing, however, compared to what happened one fateful Saturday.

"I think we'll register the boys in organized hockey this year," my father announced.

I too expected to play.

"Girls aren't allowed to play hockey in town," my father said.

How could this be? I had always played hockey with my brothers. The next weekend I stood in the driveway, tears in my eyes, while Dad loaded the boys into our old Studebaker and drove off into the big, bustling town of Cobourg to sign the necessary forms and pay required fees. That winter, I watched with my mother on the outside of the boards while my brothers zoomed over the ice, experiencing the thrill of victory, the agony of defeat.

"Why can't girls play?" I asked one day.

"It's just the way things are," my mother explained.

This exclusion was one of the great disappointments of my childhood.

My great letdown did serve a valuable purpose, however. It was an initiation of sorts, a defining moment in the arena of life. I came to an abrupt realization that male and female opportunities were not necessarily the same.

Eventually, I did get to play organized hockey, helping start a women's team during my final year at university. It was even more exciting and fulfilling than I had anticipated.

It was only a club team, not a varsity squad like the boys had. That meant we had to pay our own way. But that was okay. At least we finally got to play. Although we never won a game that year, in our minds, we had scored a major victory.[53]

* * *

Upon reading my newly published story, I felt tears welling up in my eyes. I forced them back behind the blue line. I'd initially wondered why God wanted me to write this story. Now I sensed that He was peeling back some of my thickened outer onion skin, exposing a few subtle layers of hurt from the past. As far as women and the church were concerned, I'd grown to accept that this was just the way things were. God wanted

---

[53] Judi Peers, "The Arena of Life," *Chicken Soup for the Soul: Hooked on Hockey: 101 Stories about the Players Who Love the Game and the Families that Cheer Them On* (Cos Cob, CT: Chicken Soup for the Soul Publishing, 2012), 26–28.

me to get in tune with how I felt deep in my subconscious before I began writing His book about women and the church and His heart for harmony—the book I would get serious about soon, I promised Him, but not until after Christmas, for it was our turn to host the extended Peers family on December 25.

December, no doubt, would be a write-off.

There's an old musician's joke: What's the difference between a fiddle and a violin? You don't spill beer on a violin! Now the real answer is slightly more complicated, but that joke just about sums it up: a violin is "fancy" and a fiddle is "folksy." Other than that they're pretty much the same thing.

—Megan Romer, author

seventeen

IN HIS IMAGE

As preschoolers, our three children often amazed and amused us with their delightful verbal expressions, as all young children do. One sunny afternoon, while driving by the large smokestacks of St. Mary's Cement Plant just south of Highway 401 near Bowmanville, Ontario, Stephen's countenance grew bright.

"L… lo… look, Mom!" he exclaimed, mouth forming an "O" as he directed his tiny index finger skyward. "A cloud factory!"

On another occasion, our petite dark-haired daughter came running into the kitchen in great distress. "Stephen punched me," she cried, hoping to gain sympathy and support from her parents.

"No, I didn't!" Stephen quickly assured us, shaking his carrot-coloured head from side to side as he followed closely behind his tearful little sister. "Sarah ran into my fist!"

Michael, our youngest, had the cutest expression regarding time. If asked to do a small chore, he would try and buy himself a few more minutes of playtime. "In a few whiles," he would say, voice soft and persuasive, head cocked ever so slightly, blonde curls bouncing. I loved his unique wording and smooth delivery, so I purposely avoided correcting this faulty phraseology for quite some time.

Finally, in January 2013, approximately three and a half years after God first prompted me, I found "a few whiles" to work on the book regarding women and the church. But just when the sap of inspiration was running smooth and strong and I had worked out a sweet production schedule, my husband and I booked another holiday. Since his well-deserved retirement, this has become our winter routine. We head south for a month, making the journey itself a major part of the fun, exploring a prominent city on both the going (Atlanta, this year) and the return (Charleston).

At the time of booking, I had no idea that the history of slavery would become a focal point of our travels. Acting upon the advice of good friends, we did prebook a night at a beautiful bed-and-breakfast in Georgetown, South Carolina, a former rice plantation complete with original, though dilapidated, slave quarters. I was planning to briefly address the issue of slavery near the end of my book as further proof that none of the Bible was written in a cultural vacuum.

While in Ephesus, we discovered that one of the jobs of the slaves was to sit and warm the marble seats of the latrine before their master's supposedly more valuable buttocks sat upon it. Although acknowledging man's equality in the eyes of God, Paul didn't preach against this servitude. He merely instructed both slaves and masters to work together in such a way as to promote harmony.

Consider these words of Paul:

> *Slaves, obey your masters with respect and fear, and with sincerity of heart, just as you would obey Christ. Obey them not only to win their favour when their eye is on you, but like slaves of Christ, doing the will of God from your heart. Serve whole-heartedly, as if you were serving the Lord, not men, because you know that the Lord will reward everyone for whatever good he does, whether he is slave or free. And masters, treat your slaves in the same way. Do not threaten them, since you know that he who is both their Master and yours is in heaven, and there is no favoritism with him.* (Ephesians 6:5–9)

I know Paul would take an entirely different approach to the issue of slavery if writing to the church in North America today. As stated previously, a great deal of biblical interpretation has to contend with cultural context. With the guidance and wisdom of the Holy Spirit, we must filter and interpret the influence of the cultural setting upon the words of the Holy Bible, which isn't always an easy thing to do.[54]

Before abandoning Canadian cold, ice, and snow for warmer, more southerly climes, my husband purchased an Atlanta CityPASS for both of us, giving us the right to visit five tourist hotspots at a reduced rate. Once settled in, we toured the downtown highlights: the Georgia Aquarium, the Coca-Cola Museum, and CNN's global news headquarters. If we wanted to squeeze maximum value out of our passes and use them on our final day in the city, according to the fine print, we needed to make a decision between Zoo Atlanta and the Atlanta History Center. We were divided, so we allowed the weather to cast the deciding vote: a warm, comfortable temperature on the morrow would mean a visit to the zoo while cool, damp weather would give a nod to the History Center, which also included entry to Pulitzer-Prize-winning author Margaret Mitchell's apartment in downtown Atlanta, which she had affectionately nicknamed "The Dump." I stopped in here later while Dave waited in the car, sat at her desk, and wondered what it would be like to pen a manuscript that sold over a million copies in its first six months.

Unbeknownst to us, the History Center was hosting a large temporary exhibit entitled "Slavery at Jefferson's Monticello: How the Word Is Passed Down." This display traced the history of six families enslaved on the magnificent Virginian mixed crop and tobacco plantation built by Thomas Jefferson, third president of the United States and draftsman of the Declaration of Independence.

The Declaration itself contains a few of the most famous, most celebrated words passed down in the English language.

> We hold these truths to be self-evident, that all men are created equal, that they are endowed by their Creator with certain unalienable Rights, and among these are Life, Liberty and the pursuit of Happiness.[55]

---

[54] Heated toilet seats are quite lovely, by the way. I experienced this luxury firsthand several years ago during a more-than-heartwarming visit to Japan.

[55] *The Charters of Freedom*, "Declaration of Independence." Accessed: September 17, 2014 (http://www.archives.gov/exhibits/charters/declaration_transcript.html).

A similar viewpoint was expressed by Paul in his letter to the Colossians around 62 A.D. Although bound by chains during his imprisonment in Rome, he wrote,

Do not lie to each other, since you have taken off your old self with its practices and have put on the new self, which is being renewed in knowledge in the image of its Creator. Here there is no Greek or Jew, circumcised or uncircumcised, barbarian, Scythian, slave or free, but Christ is all, and is in all. (Colossians 3:9–11)

Despite his statement regarding the equality of all men, in the same letter Paul instructs the slaves to obey their earthly masters.

Slaves, obey your earthly masters in everything; and do it, not only when their eye is on you and to win their favor, but with sincerity of heart and reverence for the Lord. (Colossians 3:22)

As in Ephesus, he's promoting harmony within the cultural constraints of one's community until all such human designations are removed not by force, but by union with Christ, liberating mankind to walk in the glorious freedom of a righteous and others-centred life. A servant life. A second fiddle kind of life.

For we do not preach ourselves, but Jesus Christ as Lord, and ourselves as your servants for Jesus' sake. For God, who said, "Let light shine out of darkness," made his light shine in our hearts to give us the light of the knowledge of the glory of God in the face of Christ. (2 Corinthians 4:5–6)

Paul approached the women's issue in the same manner: *"There is neither Jew nor Greek, slave nor free, male nor female, for you are all one in Christ Jesus"* (Galatians 3:28). Only when we are one in Christ can God's image within us be restored and renewed. This image, effaced by the fall (Genesis 3:16–19), effectively restored by Christ (Colossians 3:1–11), will one day be complete (1 John 3:1–2). All of God's creation is in the process of becoming. This is the paradox that Paul addresses. And the cultural milieu that Thomas Jefferson lived in; he kept 130 slaves at Monticello.

Although the stories featured in "Slavery at Jefferson's Monticello" were riveting and the artifacts intriguing, what impacted me most powerfully was a detailed poster depicting the deck layout of the slave ship *Brookes*. Initially released in 1788 by the Plymouth Chapter of the Society for Effecting the Abolition of the Slave Trade, this sketch is now considered an iconic symbol of the horrifying inhumanity of the Middle Passage, the leg of the triangular trade route that brought black Africans across the Atlantic to the Caribbean or the Americas.

According to the Regulated Slave Trade Act of 1788, the following space allotments were required: six feet by one foot, four inches for each man; five feet, ten inches by one foot, four inches for each woman; five feet by one foot, two inches for each child. This standardization of spacing allowed the *Brookes* to stow approximately 454 slaves.[56] On more than one occasion, however, before the act was enforced, this particular ship shackled over six hundred slaves. I'd felt terribly uncomfortable for a couple of hours on that crammed flight home from Rome. Yet it was nothing in comparison to *this*. There are no words to adequately describe the plight of the passengers chained in the lower decks of the *Brookes*.

Sharks would often swim behind the vessel, waiting with anticipation for dead bodies to be tossed starboard or portside. Poor diet, intolerable conditions, and close confinement led to diseases such as scurvy and gangrene. Dehydration was always a danger, fuelled by fever and dysentery, or simply by a shortage of suitable drinking water. Some slaves committed suicide. A model of this ship was passed on to William Wilberforce, who displayed it in the British House of Commons during his campaign to abolish the slave trade.

After entering the gallery, the first visual I came upon was the poster of the *Brookes* and I was transfixed. Initially incredulous. Then incredibly incensed. How could anyone treat their fellow human beings in such a cruel, barbaric manner? I was unable to contain my emotions as I moved

---

[56] *Wikipedia*, "Brookes (ship)." Accessed September 17, 2014 (http://en.wikipedia.org/wiki/brookes_[ship]).

through the rest of the exhibit, reading the poignant personal stories of the enslaved and viewing the artifacts reflecting their lives of bondage. Tears flowed freely. So much for not crying in public! I lingered for a couple of minutes in front of the final vignette with my back toward the others in the room, not so much to reflect upon the words or view the display more intently, but to cry privately. And then to inhale deeply, to slowly breathe in and out, in and out, hoping to take captive my emotions before catching up to my husband and moving on to the next gallery. How could anyone possibly justify such inhumanity?

The girl manning the exit door smiled empathetically as I departed and then, unexpectedly, God shared with me His heart. I was taken aback. Unhinged by the One who hinged the history of time itself.

"This is how I feel about the church's treatment of my daughters."

What? I must have misinterpreted or misheard this whisper of the Holy Spirit. Or somehow imagined this. Sure, sexual slavery, I could understand that. The degradation and despair faced by women the world over who've been abducted or tricked into a life of prostitution and shame. Or young children who've been denied their innocence by being forced or sold into child labour, or kidnapped, then intimidated and transformed into soldiers in war-torn Africa. But the church's treatment of women? How could that possibly compare?

"I hate all oppression," God explained.

Once again, I was overwhelmed by the force of God's feelings regarding this issue. This was not what we Christians call a Godwink, a sweet, subtle slice of serendipity. I was stopped-in-my-tracks Godsmacked! My whole body was shaken to its core. I found the nearest restroom, sat behind a cubicle, and let the tears flow once again; God's grief over His bride's treatment of His beloved daughters mingled with my own regarding my half-hearted response to His call to write.

Finally, I wiped the tears from my eyes, drew a few more deep breaths, and vowed to finish the book as soon as possible. If God feels this strongly, this adamantly about the women's issue, no matter my reluctance, despite my dread of appearing presumptuous, I had to discard my self-imposed shackles and get to work. People needed to know.

My husband was starting a renovation project for my daughter and her husband as soon as we got home, so I'd have a significant block of time. But I wasn't planning on mentioning anything about this Godstop here at the Atlanta History Center; people would think I was sensationalizing.

No doubt you've noticed I changed my mind. Seconds after sharing this incident with my ladies' prayer group one Tuesday morning, the Holy Spirit rewarded me, reinforced the telling, removing my reticence by immediately empowering me and my prayers with His awesome presence. I concluded that if He was this happy I'd told four of His daughters about our emotional encounter, I must document it for the benefit of thousands more.

Homeward bound from Florida, we came across the *Brookes* poster once again, this time on the wall of the Old Slave Mart located at 6 Chalmers Street, Charleston. This building was a short walking distance from our quaint inn in the well-preserved historical district of the "most beautiful city in the world," according to readers of *Condé Nast Traveler*, a premier travel magazine. We too were impressed; both of us agreed that Charleston belongs on everybody's bucket list.

This antebellum slave auction gallery, ironically located between what was at the time a Sunday School depository and a large theological library, has been turned into a museum. Wandering through this space, listening to the voices of the past (the heart-wrenching accounts of three slaves auctioned here have been recorded on tape) and viewing horrifying artifacts of bondage and torture, again evoked strong emotion. I took note of a quote by Dr. Maya Angelou, author and civil rights activist: "History, despite its wrenching pain, cannot be unlived, but if faced with courage need not be lived again." I paused for a few seconds and asked God for His courage, just a small portion of the courage and spunk He gave many of the slaves whose stories were told within those walls, those who managed to retain their human spirit despite such degradation.

For as long as I live, I'll find it hard to fathom how the institution of slavery could flourish here in North America, "land of the free, home of the brave." Yet in 1860, according to information gleaned in the Old Slave Mart, fifty-seven percent of South Carolina residents were enslaved blacks. Nor can I comprehend that during the Civil War (1861–1865), many of the Christians of the south used Paul's biblical writings to justify this institution. In fact, each side in the battle strongly believed God was on their side, as did many who supported segregation and keeping Jackie Robinson out of Major League Baseball. Years from now, I think it will be the same regarding women in the church. After a rousing sermon delivered by a female preacher come Sunday morning, or perhaps Saturday night, our grandchildren will exclaim, "Can you actually believe our grandparents thought women were to be silent in the church?"

In the meantime, there's an equally strong polarization regarding women and the church. Both sides believe God is on their side, and both groups quote scripture to support their view. According to complementarians, God created men and women equal, but a woman's role is to complement the man by subordinating herself to his leadership or headship.

Stanley J. Grenz and Denise Muir Kjesbo, authors of *Women in the Church*, are committed to what is known as the equalitarian position, which they outline as follows:

> Egalitarians seek to replace the hierarchical ordering of male over female with a focus on reciprocal relations and mutuality in relationships. In contrast to the claim set forth by complementarians that God created the second gender specifically to complement the first, egalitarians argue that God intends that men and women mutually support each other in all dimensions of life, including within the church and the church's ministry.[57]

"I guess writing this book makes me an equalitarian," I mumbled to myself while walking into my bedroom a few minutes after reading about this great divide. I'd always considered myself somewhere between the two positions.

---

[57] Grenz and Muir Kjesbo, *Women in the Church* (Downers Grove, IL: InterVarsity Press, 1995), 18.

"You are both," the Holy Spirit quickly responded. "All are equal, created to complement one another."

Once again, I marvelled at the simplicity, the clarity, the wisdom of God.

Indeed, there are far more important matters for the church to be worried about than keeping women submissive and silent. Matters that both men and women need to speak out against in a strong, unified voice.

Not long ago, I received an email notifying the Peterborough Christian community about an upcoming documentary on human trafficking, *Nefarious: Merchant of Souls*. Apparently human trafficking is the fastest growing criminal activity in the world. I was shocked by the statistics quoted by Reverend Brenda Mann, who publicized the event on behalf of Canadian Baptist Women of Ontario and Quebec.

- Governments estimate there are twenty-seven million slaves being held worldwide…
- As many as 2 million children are subjected to prostitution in the global commercial sex trade.[58]
- After drug trafficking, trafficking in humans ties with the illegal arms industry as the second largest criminal industry in the world today. It is the fastest growing criminal industry.[59]

World Vision Canada recently launched its "No Child for Sale" campaign. Their website states that 1.2 million children are sold into slavery every year.[60] How this must break the heart of God!

Slavery of any kind denies the fact that we're all made in His image. Those working the slave auction gallery in Charleston furthered this inhumanity, using labels such as "bucks" and "wenches." French philosopher Baron Montesquieu (1689–1755) once affirmed,

---

[58] *Exodus Cry*, "Some Statistics." Accessed: September 20, 2014 (*nefariousdocumentary. com/wp-content/uploads/2010/12/human-trafficking-statistics-sheet.pdf*).
[59] Ibid.
[60] World Vision Canada, "No Child for Sale." Accessed: September 17, 2014 (http:// nochildforsale.ca).

It is impossible to allow that the negroes are men; because, if we allowed them to be men, it will begin to be believed that we ourselves are not Christians.[61]

I've often wondered what being made in the image of God entails. What does *imagio Dei* really mean?

Then God said, "Let us make man in our image, in our likeness, and let them rule over the fish of the sea and the birds of the air, over the livestock, over all the earth, and over all the creatures that move along the ground. So God created man in his own image, in the image of God he created him; male and female he created them. (Genesis 1:26–27)

The phrase "let us" refers to the triune nature of our Creator God. Writing in *Community 101: Reclaiming the Local Church as a Community of Oneness*, Gilbert Bilezikian notes:

God was displeased with the fact that the man was alone (Gen. 2:18). There was one solitary individual, but he had no oneness because there was no one else with whom he could be together in oneness (2:20). Since God is Trinity, he is plurality in oneness. Therefore, the creation in his image required the creation of a plurality of persons. God's supreme achievement was not the creation of a solitary man, but the creation of human community.[62]

Initially, this statement seems to indicate that the concept of male and female is the most vital part of being created in the image of God, but this cannot be the case, for most of nature, including the animal and plant kingdoms, have this same gender dichotomy. Bilezikian explains,

---

[61] *Wikipedia*, "Baron Montesquieu." Accessed: September 17, 2014 (http://en.wikiquote.org/wiki/Montesquieu).

[62] Gilbert Bilezikian, *Community 101, Reclaiming the Local Church as a Community of Oneness* (Grand Rapids, MI: Zondervan Publishing House, 1997), 19.

When God proceeded to create "man" in his image, the recipients of the image were both male and female (1:26–27). The image of God pertained to their humanity rather than to their gender. Since God is spirit, he is not a sexual being. Therefore, he is not bound within his nature by the confinements of gender differentiations. The divine image certainly includes both maleness and femaleness. But it includes much more since it defines everything human that is different from the rest of creation. In particular, the image refers to the fact that God is a divine community of oneness, who creates a human community of oneness as his supreme achievement.[63]

In *The Knowledge of the Holy*, A.W. Tozer says that thought and speech are God's gifts to man. Sarah Young takes this thought further in her beautiful leather-bound volume *Jesus Calling*, a daily devotional documenting the result of her learning to listen to God:

Keep your focus on Me. I have gifted you with amazing freedom, including the ability to choose the focal point of your mind. Only the crown of My creation has such remarkable capability; this is a sign of being *made in My image*.[64]

Swiss theologian Karl Barth feels it is our capacity to create and nurture relationships that makes us like God, while others point to humankind's call to rule and have dominion over the rest of creation. Most biblical scholars feel that being made in God's image involves moral, intellectual, and creative capabilities and the capacity to love deeply, the ability to know and be fully known—and ultimately, to know God Himself, as I have learned from personal experience. God has clearly revealed His heart to me, evidence that part of being made in His image involves the ability to feel and share deep emotion.

---

[63] Ibid., 22.

[64] Sarah Young, *Jesus Calling: Enjoying Peace in His Presence* (Nashville, TN: Thomas Nelson Publishers, 2011), 30.

No doubt, a complexity of characteristics formulates the *imagio Dei*. Personally, I believe mankind's creative potential, our ability to interact with our world in aesthetic ways, is a significant part of being made in God's image. We mentioned earlier that breath denotes creativity in the Hebrew. As opposed to merely speaking mankind's existence into being, as He did the rest of creation (Genesis 1), one of the details of the creation account specific to mankind is the fact that God Himself breathed into Adam's nostrils *"the breath of life"* (Genesis 2:7), the potential for not only a creative, but an eternal life. Only God

> creates *ex nihilo*. But we have been given the ability and permission to manipulate, reform and build with the elements of that creation. In fact, we are expected to do so.[65]

God delights when we become co-creators with He who is our Creator.

In the Old Testament, we are told that the Holy Spirit plays a key role in artistic expression.

> *Then Moses said to the Israelites, "See, the LORD has chosen Bezalel son of Uri, the son of Hur, of the tribe of Judah, and he has filled him with the Spirit of God, with skill, ability and knowledge in all kinds of crafts—to make artistic designs for work in gold, silver and bronze, to cut and set stones, to work in wood and to engage in all kinds of artistic craftsmanship. And he has given both him and Oholiab son of Ahisamach, of the tribe of Dan, the ability to teach others. He has filled them with skill to do all kinds of work as craftsmen, designers, embroiderers in blue, purple and scarlet yarn and fine linen, and weavers—all of them master craftsmen and designers. (Exodus 35:30–35)*

The breath of God is His creative power, and that power is the Holy Spirit. How exciting to think that we have access to that creative power today. Ultimately, however, and most importantly, once we become

---

[65] Phil Vanderveen, "The Arts As Worship," *cmAlliance.ca*, Spring (2001), 20.

children of God, His Spirit and the resurrection life of His only begotten Son are creatively and continually at work in us, conforming us to His image (2 Corinthians 3:18).

And just what is involved in that image as far as gender is concerned? Well, we could take the more academic *her*meneutical approach and study the original Hebrew and Greek references to the Holy Spirit, determining how many are feminine and which ones are masculine. Perhaps pontificate on the significance of the personification of wisdom in Proverbs 8. We could analyze the female metaphors for God found in our Holy Bible and determine which ones are suitable and which ones are a little too feminist-sounding for our particular congregations. We could draw attention to the fact that both the Hebrew word *Shekinah,* representing the glory of God, and *Ruah,* the Spirit, are female nouns. Or we can simply enjoy the creative expression of the *imago Dei* found in Rembrandt's famous Spirit-inspired painting "The Return of the Prodigal Son," and leave the mystery and wonder of it all in our capable Creator's hands. In so doing, we can focus our attention on knowing and pursuing intimate relationship with He who is beyond all human understanding.

Rembrant's original rendering of the beloved parable (Luke 15:11–32) was purchased by Catherine the Great of Russia in 1766 and placed in the Hermitage in St. Petersburg. Viewing this work of art is currently on my bucket list. The painting is actually more about the love, compassion, and forgiveness of the father than the return of the son. It's a fitting representation of our loving Heavenly Father, who, with arms wide open, welcomes the homecoming of even His most errant child.

God is first and foremost our Father. Jesus acknowledged this when He assumed our human form and dwelt amongst us. The New Testament is full of such examples (Matthew 28:19; Mark 8:38; Luke 23:46; Luke 24:49; John 14:6; John 17:20–26). And we cannot forget, of course, the most famous Father reference of all time:

This, then, is how you should pray: Our Father who art in heaven, hallowed be your name, your kingdom come, your will be done on earth as it is in heaven. (Matthew 6:9–10)

As an additional aside, for some reason I can't envision a two-tiered system of worship or participation in the glorious presence of our Father who art in Heaven, whose will it is to see the heavenly pattern established here upon the earth.

It was Henri Nouwen who first brought my attention to the brilliant *Dei* detail in Rembrandt's portrayal of the Father, found within the circle of light in the true centre of the painting—in the delicate dance of illumination in the rendering of the Father's hands, where "mercy becomes flesh."[66] One can easily miss this thought-provoking nuance, unless it's pointed out, as Nouwen so elequently does in his book, *The Return of the Prodigal Son: A Story of Homecoming*:

> It all began with the hands. The two are quite different. The father's left hand touching the son's shoulder is strong and muscular. The fingers are spread out and cover a large part of the prodigal son's shoulder and back. I can see a certain pressure, especially in the thumb. That hand seems not only to touch, but, with its strength, also to hold. Even though there is a gentleness in the way the father's left hand touches his son, it is not without a firm grip.
>
> How different is the father's right hand! This hand does not hold or grasp. It is refined, soft, and very tender. The fingers are close to each other and they have an elegant quality. It lies gently upon the son's shoulder. It wants to caress, to stroke, and to offer consolation and comfort. It is a mother's hand...
>
> As soon as I recognized the difference between the two hands of the father, a new world of meaning opened up for me. The father is not simply a great patriarch. He is mother as well as father... He is, indeed, God, in whom both manhood and womanhood, fatherhood and motherhood, are fully present.[67]

---

[66] Henri J.M. Nouwen, *The Return of the Prodigal Son: A Story of Homecoming* (New York, NY: Image Books, 1994), 96.

[67] Ibid., 98–99.

Christ is the melody, the harmony, the rhythm, the tempo
and the music behind all things.

—Leonard Sweet and Frank Viola, authors

eighteen

THE RIVER OF LIFE

My husband and our two sons are putting our dock in the river today. Over the winter, the golden brown hue of the cedar has weathered to a soft rustic grey, blending perfectly with the board and batten on the exterior of the house. Although this much-anticipated event is taking place a few weeks later than last year, the water is colder because of a reluctant spring. Hip waders hiked to the hilt, my boys are experiencing what the Greek philosopher Heraclitus noted around 500 BC: "No man ever steps in the same river twice, for fresh waters are ever flowing over you." Heraclitus, a native of Ephesus, is famous for his emphasis on the flux and flow of life. Many versions of his river quote can be found floating around the internet. My favourite: "The river you step into is not the same river you are standing in."

The Israelite priests were thankful this was the case when they triumphantly carried the Ark of the Covenant across the Jordon River into the Promised Land.

Joshua said to the Israelites, "Come here and listen to the words of the Lord your God... See, the ark of the covenant of the Lord of all the earth will go into the Jordon ahead of you. Now then, choose twelve men from the tribes of Israel, one from each tribe. And as soon as the priests who carry the ark of the Lord—the Lord of all the earth—set foot in the Jordon, its waters flowing downstream will be cut off and stand up in a heap. So when the people broke camp to cross the Jordon, the priests carrying the ark of the covenant went ahead of them. Now the Jordon is at flood stage all during harvest. Yet as soon as the priests who carried the ark reached the Jordon and their feet touched the water's edge, the water from upstream stopped flowing... The priests who carried the ark of the covenant of the Lord stood firm on dry ground in the middle of the Jordon, while all Israel passed by until the whole nation had completed the crossing on dry ground. (Joshua 3:9–17)

The priests needed to take action, to obey God and step out of their comfort zone into the strong-swelling current in order to experience His presence in an amazing way. Temporarily dammed, the Jordon River functioned in the same miraculous manner as the Red Sea forty years before. I always remind myself of this story when God assigns me an unexpected, out-of-the-norm, into-the-storm assignment. I've thought of it often as I worked on this book.

We haven't witnessed anything this spectacular while living here on the edge of the river Otonabee (an Ojibwa word meaning "flashing waters running swiftly"), but one of the things we love best about our new location is the constant of change—not only from season to season, but day to day. Even in midwinter, the river is ever-altering, always adjusting to the fluctuating circumstances of life.

Large irregular-shaped sheets of ice flow swiftly by our living room windows one January afternoon. The next morning, due to warmer temperatures, steam rises, hovering over the surface of the water, creating an ethereal, theatrical effect. Periodically, the river freezes. Come spring, water levels are in a perpetual state of flux as spring runoff affects the local watershed and lock masters receive their orders and work to regulate the flow between the tri-lakes (Pigeon, Buckhorn, and Chemong), and the more shallow waters of Rice Lake, in preparation for the upcoming navigational season. Once that launches, an eclectic, entertaining mix of pleasure craft cruise the channel on the opposite side of the river: small runabouts, fishing boats, multimillion dollar cruisers, houseboats, family-filled pontoon boats, the occasional noisy, cigarette boat, Liftlock tour boats, the massive *Kawartha Voyageur* with its retractable bow, and sailboats too, their motors dropped in order to safely traverse the serpentine river. Most captains pay careful attention to the swaying red and green channel markers. Those who don't up the level of excitement and adventure for us folk who dwell onshore.

Here on the river, wildlife abounds. Great blue herons, usually content to stand stoic on a rock, dock, or log, occasionally surprise and delight, jerkily high-strutting their stuff along our small beachfront. Large families of Canada geese paddle by, black and white heads held majestically high. By (or bye) being the key word here, for no one wants their property chosen for a latrine. The level of excrement each goose produces is astounding—up to one and a half pounds per day. In early spring, ducks frequently fight, while muskrats play, chasing each other around one of our submerged tree trunks. And the fish! Bass, pickerel, and muskellunge! But we're diligent to practice catch-and-release so our grandchildren's children will be able to enjoy the same fishing fun someday.

All this natural beauty and wonder came together in an interesting vignette one evening this April. A massive ice storm hit southern Ontario, breaking off the branches of several trees and taking out power lines. This was an inconvenience, but at the same time the beauty that accompanied the storm was breathtaking. Trees, burnished by ice, glistened gloriously in the sun. Grasses, lining riverbanks and roadways, temporarily disguised their weedy mantles by donning new jewel-encrusted cloaks. Wire fences, humbly staking out the boundaries of their masters' fields, usually unworthy of a second glance, were transformed into exquisite works of art. Unfortunately, several trees draping the shore, weary with the weight of the ice, lost significant limbs. For the next few days, a flotilla of Mother Nature's flotsam drifted down the river.

A couple nights after the storm, while barbequing on our upper deck celebrating the first breath of summer, I noticed a good-sized branch travelling against the flow, making its way upstream. A considerable wake, one worthy of the finest seafaring vessel, rippled out from behind. What was going on?

As the branch made its way closer to my vantage point, I discovered that a furry brown animal functioned as its propeller. Was it a muskrat?

A river otter? A beaver? I called my nephew Ryan to come and take a look. Most likely a beaver doing a bit of heavy lumbering, we decided, gathering materials for the construction of a dam—just one more example of the rich diversity we now experience as a result of living on the Otonabee.

Change is a constant on the river. In the broader scheme of things, one could say that change is the river of life. God is the same yesterday, today, and forever, for He is the only immutable one. But when it comes to life, when it comes to culture, the only constant is change. The world we were born into is not the world we are living in. My mother-in-law, Simonne Peers, turns ninety-six next week. The changes she has seen in the course of her lifetime are astounding! Change is inevitable—unless of course, you're standing in front of a vending machine.

Granted, change isn't always synonymous with progress. As Christians, if we're serious about our faith and obedient to our God, we'll often find ourselves in the position of that large brown beaver, paddling against the flow with the intensity of an Olympic rower going for gold—stopgapping the cultural shifts that are detrimental to society, curbing current trends toward narcissistic individualism, overly materialistic consumerism, and moral decay.

Morality, according to C.S. Lewis, involves three things:

> Firstly, with fair play and harmony between individuals. Secondly, with what might be called tidying up or harmonizing the things inside each individual. Thirdly, with the general purpose of human life as a whole: what man was made for: what course the whole fleet ought to be on: what tune the conductor of the band wants it to play.[68]

When the symphony is out of sync with the conductor, when the ship sails off-course, merrily meandering outside the channel markers placed for its own well-being and safety, when society starts playing its own tune, ignoring its Creator, when shameful, degrading practices like human trafficking are on the rise, radical change is in order. Howard

---

[68] C.S. Lewis, *Mere Christianity* (London, UK: Harper Collins Publishers, 1997), 59.

Marshall, a biblical scholar of note who specializes in the pastoral epistles, says, "The gospel does not change, but our perception of it may need revision."[69] Our traditional perception of women in ministry may need revising if the church is to successfully combat the increasing tide of moral decay.

Sue Augustine, writing in *Simple Retreats for a Women's Soul*, provides evidence that questioning the status quo can sometimes prove profitable:

> A little girl noticed that her mother always cut the ends from the ham before placing it in the roasting pan. When she asked why, her mother explained that her own mother had always done it. So the child asked her grandmother, who said she was simply following her mother's example. Finally, her great-grandmother solved the mystery when she admitted to cutting the ends off the ham because her old roasting pan was too small![70]

Many churches, in the restrictions they place on women in ministry, aren't merely cutting off the ends; they're discarding the main body. More than half (some estimate sixty to sixty-five percent) of Jesus' followers are female. Tossing away that much apostolic, prophetic, evangelistic, and pastoral potential seems ridiculous in light of our current cultural situation—that of increasing darkness. God wants to mobilize His full army, to train and utilize His entire team.

In preparation for writing this book, I visited a number of churches that embrace the full participation of women. I didn't feel these churches were acting in opposition to God's Word or His will. In fact, the reverse was the case; a tangible sense of God's Spirit prevailed. Furthermore, not only did these congregations foster an inclusive environment for women and help combat the church's subtle teaching of the superiority of men, but they placed an emphasis on increased participation by all. And there was a greater focus on prayer!

---

[69] Alan F. Johnson, ed., *How I Changed My Mind About Women in Leadership: Compelling Stories from Prominent Evangelicals* (Grand Rapids, MI: Zondervan Publishing House, 2010), 43.

[70] Sue Augustine, *Simple Retreats for a Woman's Soul* (Eugene, OR: Harvest House Publishers, 2001), 169.

This hadn't always been the case, as these churches had to work through the issue of women in ministry at some point in their history. Pastor Frank Patrick, formerly of Calvary Pentecostal Church, in Peterborough, Ontario, recalls an interesting incident:

> When I began to broaden the role of women in our church over twenty years ago, I asked three women to help distribute the elements one Sunday morning. Traditionally, six men would handle that.
>
> One elderly man sitting near the front of the church folded his arms in a gesture of defiance and proclaimed, "I'll not take communion from the hands of a woman."
>
> The church fell into an awkward silence until another congregant suddenly spoke up. "I'll bet you'll take your supper from the hands of a woman."

Despite my initial reluctance to tackle the issue, I'm confident God has entrusted me with this message for His church, the bride of Christ. He is awakening the women of this world, pouring out His Spirit upon His beloved daughters as He declared in His Word (Acts 2:17–18). He announced His plans to women at many pivotal points in history (Jesus' birth, Luke 1:26–35; His resurrection, John 20:14–17). Why not now, at this critical juncture? God is calling and empowering His precious daughters to not only stand up and be counted for His Kingdom, but to speak boldly of Him, to write creatively with Him, to pray and prophesy with Holy Spirit power, and to proclaim His Son as *"the way, the truth and the life"* (John 14:6).

God irrupts into His world in a manner befitting its cultural setting. In dealing with ancient Israel, He established a covenant similar to political treaties in the ancient Near East. During first-century Christendom, He instructed Paul to advise the church to respect its hierarchical framework while pointing to a better way. The audience Paul addressed is not the audience God is speaking to today; Jesus' incarnation birthed a redemptive, transformational process, setting in motion the elevation of women to a position of freedom and equality, a position enjoyed in God's original creation. This is a concept that North American culture as a whole is learning to accept. At the same time, unfortunately, it's using the church's refusal to change its attitude toward women as justification for the rejection of its more important teachings. The church is cited as being out of date, archaic even.

Today, God is calling for the church to embrace

- a paradigm shift,
- a fence moving,
- an inclusive invitation to the dance.

He desires that all His children have opportunity to fully participate in the arena of life. Our Creator God wants to conduct an orchestra of second fiddles, all in tune, in perfect pitch, harmonizing with one another and resonating with His Son, the One He has chosen to play first. Only then will we become instruments fit for His purposes (Romans 6:13).

John Stott (1921–2011), a leader of the worldwide evangelical movement and at one point chaplain to the queen, suggested that we preserve the "inner substance of what God is teaching, while claiming the liberty to re-clothe it in modern cultural dress."[71] The inner substance God not only desires, but delights in, is harmony—playing second fiddle to one another regardless of gender, class or race. Living a life of sacrifice and service, a life of oneness with God and with each other. A life of unity. Unity, it's been said, is the basis of the church's credibility.

Unity is not the same as uniformity. Being one doesn't mean we'll always agree. Nor does God want His children trampled upon. He desires us to live an others-centred life without losing the tempo and harmony of our own. This is what is modelled for us in the relationship of the Triune God. The Three in One—the Father, Spirit, and the Son.

The oneness Jesus speaks of for His church is of such critical importance that it is the climactic conclusion to the prayer He delivered after unexpectedly breaking into a dramatic demonstration of second fiddlin'—the washing of His disciples' feet:

---

[71] Alvera Mickelsen, ed., *Women, Authority & the Bible* (Downers Grove, IL: InterVarsity Press, 1986), 38. This book is a collection of essays and responses presented at the Evangelical Colloquium on Women and the Bible, held in 1984 in Oak Brook, Illinois.

I have given them the glory that you gave me, that they may be one as we are one. I in them and you in me. May they be brought to complete unity to let the world know that you sent me and have loved them even as you loved me. "Father, I want those you have given me to be with me where I am, and to see my glory, the glory you have given me because you loved me before the creation of the world. Righteous Father, though the world does not know you, I know you, and they know that you have sent me. I have made you known to them, and will continue to make you known in order that the love you have for me may be in them and that I myself may be in them." (John 17:22–26)

According to Leonard Sweet and Frank Viola, Christ is

the melody, the harmony, the rhythm, the tempo and the music behind all things. The heavens and the earth sing His song and play His tune.[72]

C.S. Lewis makes a similar connection:

And that, by the way, is perhaps the most important difference between Christianity and all other religions: that in Christianity God is not a static thing… but a dynamic, pulsating activity, a life, almost a kind of drama. Almost, if you will not think me irreverent, a kind of dance.[73]

This God that Lewis speaks of—the Lord of all the earth—is extending an invitation to all humanity to embrace the music and participate fully in this dance called life.

In harmonious accord with twenty-first-century culture, God not only wants to blow the lid off the box of tradition the church has placed women in (or, for that matter, anyone who is marginalized in our

---

[72] Leonard Sweet and Frank Viola, *Jesus Manifesto: Restoring the Supremacy and Sovereignty of Christ* (Nashville, TN: Thomas Nelson Publishers), 16.

[73] C. S. Lewis, *Mere Christianity* (London, UK: Harper Collins Publishers, 1997), 145.

society); He desires to dismantle the box completely and transform it into a dance floor.

Like Oscar, our friend with Down syndrome, God wants all humanity to dance while we can, to follow Him step by step, moving to the beat of His heart, using our Holy Spirit giftedness and experiencing His power. This will enrich our lives, and at the same time advance His Kingdom. For me, right now, that means obeying His voice, answering His call to write a book entitled *Playing Second Fiddle: God's Heart for Harmony Regarding Women and the Church*.

And so I do.

Live in harmony with one another. (Romans 12:16)
—Paul, apostle and author